CARVING BIRDS AND BEASTS

The best from WOODcarving magazine

CARVING BIRDS AND BEASTS

The best from WOODcarving magazine

GUILD OF MASTER CRAFTSMAN PUBLICATIONS LTD

This collection first published in 1995 by
Guild of Master Craftsman Publications Ltd,
Castle Place, 166 High Street, Lewes,
East Sussex BN7 1XU

Printed in Hong Kong by H & Y Printing Ltd.

Front cover photograph by David Tippey

CONTENTS

NOTES

Please note that names, addresses, prices etc. were correct at the time the articles were originally published, but may since have changed.

Measurements

Throughout the book instances will be found where a metric measurement has fractionally varying imperial equivalents, usually within 1/16in either way. This is because in each particular case the closest imperial equivalent has been given. A mixture of metric and imperial measurements should NEVER be used – always use either one or the other.

INTRODUCTION

Since its introduction in August 1992 *Woodcarving* magazine has become a major source of information for woodcarvers around the world. Each issue is devoted to providing information about carvers, their carvings, techniques and inspiration. The range of woodcarving is constantly expanding as new uses for this ancient craft are discovered. Woodcarving now embraces everything from large-scale monumental works, to life-sized representations of garden birds.

Until this century woodcarving meant mastering the use of traditional handtools: knives, chisels, gouges, rasps and scrapers, sharpening with bench stones and slip stones. Hand tools still have their place in the workshop, but since the 1950s and 60s power tools and machines have become more common in the workshop.

New tools, machines and accessories are being developed to satisfy the demand from a new generation of woodcarvers. Carving discs fitted to angle grinders speed the removal of large amounts of wood, and are even being used as finishing tools by the more skilled practitioners. Flexible shaft machines, fitted with a variety of cutters and burrs, are used to create details on smaller pieces such as birds and animals.

Birds and animals are probably the most popular subjects for carvings. Many carvers enjoy the challenge of producing a carving with a recognizable shape, features and proportions – capturing some vital aspect of the subject. Some try to capture an impression of the animal, by creating an abstracted sculptural form. Others reproduce their subjects exactly – so life-like that observers wait to see if the carving will move.

In this book you will find all types and styles of animal and bird carving. We have selected features, technical articles and projects from *Woodcarving* magazine that give a broad insight into all the carving methods employed today. I hope that you will enjoy reading about them and will try some of them out.

Neil Bell
Editor, *Woodcarving*

Born in 1966, on the Welsh borders where he still lives, Philip Nelson showed an interest and aptitude for carving at an early age. He presented an appreciative infant school headteacher with an owl he had sculpted from a block of wood at the age of only seven years.

He trained as a cabinetmaker but his skill in wood was better utilised in the art of waterfowl carving.

Some of his early work evoked the admiration of HRH Prince Charles in 1987. Since then his 'pieces' have become so realistic and the standard of craftsmanship so high, down to the detail of the finest feather, that one expects the birds to move and fly off as one approaches.

Philip has made decoy carving into an art appreciated by the connoisseur. His work is on display at Nature in Art, the International Centre for Wildlife Art at Twigworth, Gloucester. In this arena of the world's finest wildlife artists, his is currently the only example of decorative decoy carving which has been accepted for public exhibition. He is committee member of the British Decoy Wildfowl Carvers Association.

WILDFOWL AND HARMONY

PHILIP NELSON

A wildfowl carver who finds inspiration in birds and music.

It is known that the great Russian pianist Emil Gilels once told a hapless pupil that he was, 'playing like a policeman'. What the legendary maestro meant, of course, was that his student was playing in a way that highlighted each accent — metaphorically dotting every i and crossing all the t's — and making the music sound clinical and stupified. This interpretation robbed the music of its spontaneity and innate spirit.

It is with these thoughts in mind that I approach the task of depicting waterfowl in sculpture. It is my intention that by displaying a bird in solitude — rather than fixing it to an artificial base and surrounding it with pseudo-habitat — that I give the impression that the waterfowl form which people see before them is, in fact, a real duck. It might have somehow, quite ingeniously, arrived, and is reposing on their drawing room table.

Dead detail

To pay painstaking attention to every ornithological detail often achieves a pedantically correct carving, but the artistic aura of both the bird and its creator could be lost as a result. A bird sculpture is not diminished by the detail itself, but by an unbalanced belief that time and skill achieves great art. Detail can enhance, but may well clutter and detract from the important things, such as sculptural form and clarity of vision.

However, before starting a new piece a waterfowl artist, like a good musician, should be competent technically, and perhaps more importantly, have a thorough knowledge of the subject in question. To acquire this knowledge I visit the Wildfowl and Wetlands Trust in Lancashire. There, initially, rather than take photographs or make sketches, I study subliminally; that is visualising a finished carving the moment I catch sight of a new species.

It was said that the Duke of Wellington fought all his greatest battles whilst walking the playing fields of Eton. Similarly, I must confess that I think I have produced my best work whilst supping hot tea in the coffee shop at Martin Mere.

When my subject is chosen I do take a small number of photographs, showing the species in question usually sideways on, so that you can see through the nostrils of the bill. This type of photograph will give me the basic proportions, from which I can work. After this a suitable pose has to be found.

Canadian style

My biggest regret over the past seven years is that during the early, formative stages of my career I used other carver's ideas occasionally. Many young artists do, seeing it as a short cut to prosperity. I should now advise any artist or craftsman, in any field, against this. At worst you will be

An Atlantic
Canada goose.

accused of plagiarism, and at best you will reproduce the mistakes of others.

I regret that about six years ago, against my better judgement, I copied the pose of a pintail drake by an eminent Canadian carver. The bird was displayed at a decoy carving fair, and it sold immediately, for a four figure sum. The sale caused comment, fuelled by the fact that nothing of any note had been sold by anyone else. In the intervening years I was to discover that the Canadian carver's style was endlessly reproduced, much to my horror. I now compare this experience to one that a

successful actress might have, if she had stripped for the cameras in the early part of her career. At the time it was merely a means of progressing in a profession.

The only sure way to learn the anatomy of wildfowl, whilst developing one's artistry, is to follow the advice of Doctor David Trapnell — Director of Nature in Art, Gloucester. He advocates the study of the live subject and to draw it, draw it, and draw

it. Strong adherence to this maxim also precludes the use of clay models and taxidermist's mounts.

Solid carving

All my work is carved from a single block of English lime, with no separate head or any inserted wing or tail feathers. I choose to work in this way to avoid any accusation of model making. I feel that it is closer in spirit to the way in which great sculptors such as Michelangelo, Rodin and Camille Claudel worked.

The majority of the waste wood is removed by hand, using a 1in 25mm, out-

**Photographs by
Penny Davis.**

A pintail drake.

canal, firmer gouge and a carver's mallet. Some people might regard this as over zealous, comparable to raking the front lawn with a comb, but I enjoy the intimicy and tranquillity of the wood peeling away. I feel that I am more focused on the composition of the piece as a whole. The overall condition of carvings can be very weak, when tools such as flexidrives and rotary cutters are used.

I do the more refined shaping with a small knife, while the final detail is achieved using a ¼in 6mm swan-necked gouge. I do not resort to rows and rows of ruby carvers or dentist's bits: the acquisition of which has been compared, by one of my students, with a fisherman purchasing endless items of fishing tackle, in the forlorn hope of improving his casting, or with a golfer buying the most expensive clubs to better his handicap.

Feathers and finish

Over the years the questions I have been asked most frequently about my carvings are:

'Where do you get your feathers from?'

'How do you stick them to the wood?'

In some ways such queries are a compliment, though somewhat saddening. However, the more knowledgeable members of the public ask:

'How do you get such a soft look on all of your feathers?'

To do this. I use a pyrography machine, called 'a detailer', to burn texture lines as close as possible. The lines are cut at about

230 to the inch (even finer than on the real feathers of some of the larger birds). These lines are burned in at various depths and colour intensities from straw to a very dark brown. When painted they produce a transparent lusciousness; similar to that seen on an actual feather as sunlight is reflected from it at a distance. Beginners might find it difficult to use the detailer at its hottest setting, to produce the darker tone. The secret is to use the quickest possible flick of the wrist, and practice the technique

A garganey drake, carved from the solid, to avoid accusations and model making.

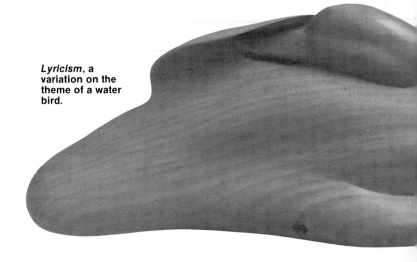

Lyricism, a variation on the theme of a water bird.

again and again on a piece of wood. When mastered, the process can produce an effect on the darker feathers far superior to that achieved by a mechanical abrasive stone. I do use some 'stoning' procedures, to texture surfaces which, when painted will be any of the paler shades around white.

I colour my sculptures using Cryla Flow paints, diluted to an almost orange-juice viscosity, so as not to mask the fine feather detail burnt in at the previous stage. I use Cryla Flow colours as they can be diluted thinly without losing their binding qualities. Also, they have a greater transparency than gouache based paints. This means that they dovetail well into my feather texturing technique.

In my experience, the use of matt colours to paint a bird which has been 'stoned' throughout, can produce a carving lacking in tonal nuances; almost ceramically opaque in appearance.

An interpretation of a diving duck.

The creation of one of my birds usually entails about three months of intense attention to detail; detail which I, the artist, feel to be important. My persistence is rewarded when I finally remove the surplus paint from around the eyeball, and see the duck come alive. It is generally the case in works of art, where human, bird or animal forms are depicted, that the eye is the most important focal point in the entire composition. It has been said that, 'the eyes are the mirror of the soul', and I find that poor eye contact in any work can destroy the presence of the piece.

Theme variation

The summer of 1992 saw a marked change in the style of some of my work, when I completed my first interpretational sculpture entitled *Lyricism*. The inspiration for this piece came from the Symphonic Studies, Opus 13, of Robert Schumann.

These are 12 studies and five variations following on from the Opus 10 Studies of Chopin, only this time Schumann developed Chopin's ideas a step further by making the set more orchestral in character. So much so that attempts have been made to transcribe the work for a full symphony orchestra, in the same way that Ravel orchestrated Mussorgsky's Pictures at an Exhibition. However in Schumann's work whilst some passages lend themselves to orchestration, others because of their unique pianistic qualities, do not, and can only have full justice done to them on the keyboard.

It was with these elements in mind, that I decided to carve a waterfowl form that would be representational to a degree in the head, neck and breast areas, but highly stylised in the wing and tail regions. There would be no way of texturing or painting the sculpture at a later stage; no chance of orchestration.

For this work I chose English lime, feeling that a wood with a more exotic grain figure would clutter the stark and simple form I was trying to produce. On completion I showed my sculpture to a London Gallery owner. He described the piece as: 'Bordering on the minimalist'.

Those readers who have persevered with me so far, will have realised that I derive a great deal of inspiration from listening to music. Indeed, one of my favourite operas is Electra by Richard Strauss. In this piece, he wrote music that was sometimes bordering on the atonal (the lack of tonal centre or established key). This, together with the gallery owner's observation, instilled in me the desire to produce a completely 'atonal sculpture': in the spirit of Schoenberg's five pieces for orchestra. A sculpture devoid of any recognisable wildfowl features, but still retaining the fundamental form of a definite type of bird.

My ambition is not to win numerous competitions, nor to acquire any great wealth through my work, but to create works that speak with the quintessential voice of Philip Nelson, and no-one else. The poet and painter William Blake asked of art whether it should be: 'confined to the sordid drudgery of facsimile, representation of merely mortal and perishing substances, and not be, as poetry and music are, elevated to its own proper sphere of invention and visionary conception?' ■

CARVING AN OTTER

REG PARSONS

THE OTTER HAS BECOME A RARE ANIMAL IN BRITAIN. THE AUTHOR SHOWS HOW TO CAPTURE ONE IN WOOD.

The otter is a solitary, secretive, aquatic animal. It is very well adapted to its aquatic way of life having a dense brown waterproof coat, webbed feet with five toes, and ears and nostrils that can be closed against the entry of water. The small ears are almost concealed in the dense fur.

The body is about 760mm 30" long, and the tail, which is flat at the botton to assist swimming, is about 510mm 20". It is now extremely rare in the south of England, and scarce elsewhere.

The wood: I used Cornish elm (Ulmus stricta) as the lovely brown colouring and the wild grain give a very realistic effect to the wiry coat in the finished work.

Any clean hard wood would be suitable, but if a realistic colouring is required and elm is not available, either oak or chestnut could be used as both contain

sufficient tannic acid to be affected by the fumes of ammonia. The finished carving could then be fumed to a realistic colour — I will describe how to do this later.

Blocking in: Thoroughly clean up the wood and examine it

closely for shakes or knots that will have to be avoided, or attractive areas of grain or figuring that can be incorporated in the design.

Produce a template from the side view drawing using a grid to

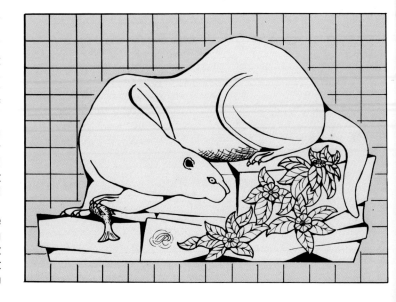

scale up to fit the available stock. Use the template to clearly mark out the side view and then remove wood from outside the lines.

Use a bandsaw if possible or else saw in radially at close intervals across the grain and split the wood away between the sawcuts with a large bosting in gouge, say a ⅝" No. 7 and woodcarvers' mallet (Photo 1).

Mark the body centre line, noting that it is not parallel with the base sides due to the shoulders being narrower than the rump. The neck and head centre line should curve realistically making full use of the block width.

Note that as the otter's tail and the fish are defined an opportunity is taken to define the rocks where it is convenient and realistic to do so (Photo 5).

The fish: Before the fish can be carved the left front leg holding it must be clearly defined. The paws have five webbed toes tipped by small non-retractable claws. The webbing is not visible in this study as the toes are positioned close together. It is important here that the claws are seen to go round the fish instead of just lying on top. They should also be made as angular as possible, each joint being clearly visible.

'It is only by close study of the otter, its shape and lifestyle, that you will bring the carving to life.'

Draw two parallel lines a body, neck, and head width apart each side of the centre line and then remove wood from above the head and the sides of the body (Photo 2).

It can be seen from this photograph that there was a bad area of dark brown soft wood in the head position that was not evident when I started the carving. This is quite common in Cornish elm grown in the wet acidic conditions of the South West, but in this case I was fortunate enough to be able to lower the head sufficiently to avoid it — indeed I think that it made the carving more dramatic (Photo 3).

Draw the rear legs and tail and define the rear leg very deeply with a quick gouge, say a ⅜" No. 10, using the same gouge to define the tail. Keep the sides flat and the edges square. Define the fish and the front legs with the same gouge (Photo 4).

Bosting in: This is the stage of the work where the carving is actually shaped. It is essential now to obtain photographs and drawings of otters and consult them closely and frequently as the work proceeds.

It seems obvious to say, but it is impossible to carve anything unless you know what it really looks like, and it is only by close study of the otter, its shape and lifestyle, that you will bring your carving to life.

Once the paw is right the fish should be shaped with the tail curving up slightly. The temptation here is to undercut the bottom of the tail where it joins the rock. This would, however, make it vulnerable to damage. A realistic effect can still be achieved even when it is attached solidly to the rock.

The detailed carving of the fish is best left to later but this is a good point for me to describe how it is carried out. The eye is too small to be satisfactorily carved, but a realistic effect can be achieved by pressing firmly into the wood a length of 3mm ⅛" DIA bar that has had a shallow spherical hole drilled in the end. The two fins are carved onto the flat surface of the rock.

Head: The head is broad and flat and the muzzle very short, with the small ears barely visible among the dense fur. The eyes are deep set and penetrating. Bost in the head as shown in Photos 5 and 6 and prepare the deep hollows for the eyes with a ¼" No. 9.

The small bright eyeball can be formed in the same way as the fish's eye but by using a larger diameter length of rod. Alternatively it can be carved by stabbing down vertically with a suitably shaped gouge, say ¼" No. 9, and then revolving the gouge to complete the circle.

The eyeball can be rounded

Photo 1 Using a saw, gouge and mallet to remove waste wood

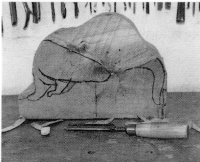
Photo 2 Initial marking and cutting out of the body

Photo 3 Head position redrawn lower and cut out

Photo 4 Fish and front legs defined

Photo 5 Further detail cut and rocks marked

Photo 6 More detail and flowers cut

Photo 7 Head and eye detail

The leaves are formed by stabbing down vertically with a suitably shaped gouge (I used a ⅝" No. 7) and the waste wood is removed with a ¼" No. 3. One side of the leaf tip is concave — stabbing down vertically with a ⅜" No. 6 will give this the right shape, and the waste wood is again removed with the ¼" No. 3.

The leaf veins are formed by pressing into the wood and indenting it with a ¼" No. 3. This should be done with the greatest restraint or the wood will split. A few of the leaf edges are also curled over to give greater realism, although this is difficult to see in the photographs.

Tail: This is very wide where it leaves the body, indeed it almost appears to be an extension of the body. It tapers towards the tip, which is still thick and wide. It is also flat underneath so it is unnecessary to undercut it to any

over with a ⅛" No. 3. The two small triangles at the front and rear of the eyeball can be cut in by making two inclined cuts with the ⅛" No. 3 or by the point of a sharp craft knife. I have found the Stanley Slimknife fitted with blade 5905 to be ideal for this, as it is for other general purpose woodcarving (Photo 7).

Base: All the rocks should now be drawn in a naturalistic way, avoiding the area covered by the flowers and leaves. Define them deeply with a quick gouge, say a ⅜" No. 10, shaping them at different angles with a ⅜" No. 3 (Photos 8 and 9).

It is important that the rocks are seen to be sitting firmly on top of one another and not give the impression that if they are touched they will tumble over. One rock should be selected at this stage with an easily visible flat area on which your mark will be carved.

Flowers and leaves: It is unlikely and unrealistic that the vegetation would lie on a perfectly flat, vertical surface, so the area on which it is intended to carve the foliage should be made rounded and undulating with a ⅝" No. 3 and then cleaned up with a scraper to a high standard of finish before marking on the flowers (Photo 6).

The flower centres are formed by stabbing down vertically with a ¼" No. 9 and then rotating the gouge to complete the circle. The ends of the petals are formed in the same way and the waste wood around them is removed with a ¼" No. 3. The flowers should then stand proud from the rocks about 5mm ³/₁₆".

The petal centres are carved concave with a ⅜" No. 6. This will also form the ridges between each petal if carefully done. Round over the centre button with a ⅛" No. 3 and mark its surface at close intervals with an icepick to indicate stamens (Photo 10).

Photo 8 Rocks detailed

Photo 9 Mark carved on a flat rock

Photo 10 Vegetation details carved

great extent, although the tip can be undercut slightly to free it from the rock. It is important not to overdo this as it will make the tip vulnerable to damage (Photo 8).

Coat: The texture of the coat was formed with a ⅛" No. 10 by making a series of cuts following the natural flow of the hair. The gouge was allowed to ride out of the wood at the end of each cut in order to give a pointed tip to the cut. Each alternate cut should be made at an angle to the previous one to give the wet coarse look.

Note that the nose is left bare and that the cuts still follow the general direction of the hair even where they cross the wrinkles formed at the turn in the neck and at the front end of the rear legs (Photo 8, 9, 10 and 11).

Finishing: Sand over the flat surface of rock previously selected for your mark and carve it on. My mark was carved with the Stanley Slimknife (Photo 9). It is well worthwhile taking some trouble over this as the design of the carving does not make it particularly vulnerable to damage and with care it should last well into the next century and beyond.

People then will want to know who the artist/craftsman was, and your mark and date will add greatly to the interest of the work and indeed its value.

Fuming: If this is necessary the fuming process is quite simple. The carving is placed in a box with its base supported above the floor of the box by four nails to allow the fumes to circulate round the carving. Saucers filled with ammonia are placed at intervals round the work but not too close or an unpleasant dark patch will result.

The colour change can be observed and then stopped when sufficient depth of colour has been achieved by simply removing the carving from the fumes. A piece of glass or plastic placed over the front of the box will enable the colour change to be

high degree of polish and this work is no exception. Yet some treatment is necessary to prevent the wood getting grubby. Coating the carving with sanding sealer will bring up the grain and colour and offer protection against dirt and water — a possible cause of future shakes.

It does also, unfortunately, destroy the lovely tactile feel of the wood which is a part of the pleasure of a wood carving, leaving the surface with a rough feel to it. An acceptable compromise is to first coat with sanding sealer and then after rubbing down with 600 grit wet and dry paper polish with a good quality wax polish. The finish will provide the protection of the sanding sealer coupled with the lovely feel and soft lustre of the wax.

Photo 11 Coat markings follow the flow of the form

monitored without exposure to the ammonia fumes which are quite unpleasant.

Fuming is a more natural and reliable method of producing a deep rich colour change than staining, the results of which can be unpredictable, particularly on carved work where there are constant changes of grain. A test piece should of course always be tried first.

Few carvings look well with a

It will be difficult to sand down this carving without sanding over crisply carved edges. I used a piece of 600 grit wet and dry about 75mm 3" x 20mm ¾" with slits cut in each end wedged into a slot cut in the end of a length of rod. When revolved at high speed in an electric drill it was just sufficient to clean up the rough areas without sanding over the edges. It had to be used with the greatest restraint, of course. ■

By observing real pelicans, it is clear that all their extraordinary features are in fact functional

A WONDERFUL BIRD

MICHAEL HENDERSON DESCRIBES THE CARVING OF HIS PELICAN, WINNER OF THE BEST IN SHOW PRIZE AT LAST YEAR'S PENSTHORPE EXHIBITION

To quote Dixon Merritt: 'A wonderful bird is the pelican: his bill will hold more than his belican'. The pelican's appearance *is* extraordinary. It is as if Nature had gone too far for once. It is a heraldic bird, and in Christian mythology stands for charity and devotion: the mother is shown piercing her breast to feed her young with her own blood.

But when you observe a real pelican you quickly see that all its extraordinary features are functional. That great beak with its curious sack underneath does not send it plummeting down head first. To fly, the bird folds up its long neck and pulls the beak towards its body. To fish, the neck unfolds rapidly and the beak and its sack scoop up fish long before the warning shadow of the bird has approached. The pelican has wide webbed feet to swim with, and huge wings with large flight feathers to carry its weight.

This meeting of the extraordinary and the actual, of Mythology and Nature, appealed to me. When I went to watch the pelicans I saw something else – a tenderness. They are social birds: they fish together in a circle surrounding their prey; they sit together and seem to need each other's company.

Look and learn

Before starting on a piece, I go into a period of doubt. It seems presumptuous to portray anything, so it must be done with respect, or wonder. I have to reduce this doubt somehow, by sketching from life, modelling in plasticine, or just plain wondering until some conviction comes.

So I went to Bristol Zoo with binoculars, a sketch book and biro and a camera with a long lens. Photographs may be useful later, but they are no substitute for looking. They do not show how the bird moves or instil a feeling for its presence.

Soon you start to identify a characteristic position that might be possible to create in wood, and to concentrate on that. It must have tension and intention. If it is too dynamic you won't be able to portray it in wood, and the piece will just look wooden. So flight, I think, should be implied in the power of wings. If the position is too static, the possibility and excitement of flight are missed, though some sleeping birds are beautiful.

I chose to show the pelican sunning itself, with one wing raised to let air around it. This position had an interesting asymmetry; it had repose but alertness; it showed the power of the wings and the great feathers as they cascaded down the back in an unruly staircase.

I must have sketched, looking through binoculars and then scribbling, for three hours and came away with about fifty little drawings. I had a sense of awe and I felt dizzy.

In Christian mythology the pelican symbolised charity and devotion. This carved stone example is on St Mary Redcliffe church, Bristol

Basic shape established, but leaving scope for change and refinement

Plain forms emphasise the sculptural quality and the wood; the detail gives the living presence of the bird

faith. At first my imaginings seem so flimsy and two-dimensional on the surfaces of the wood, but later this act of faith is rewarded when, unlike a drawing, all the surfaces begin to join and lead to the intended shape.

Carve all round: don't focus on one part. Establish the shape as a whole and cautiously find the proportions of parts within it. Resist the temptation to bandsaw

Left
Mallet and gouges are used to gradually add detail

Below
Flight is implied in the power of the wings with their huge feathers

Wood and form

A woodcarving has two elements that must be in balance – the beauty of the wood and the form. The flow of the wood and the spirit of the bird should intermingle. Any joins in the wood can break this integrity and should be avoided, or placed carefully. (Of course none of this applies if the carving is covered with opaque paint.)

The weight and strength of the wood should be appropriate for the wood and the form of the bird. Legs should not look too flimsy, or large body masses too heavy. So it is appropriate to alter what might be considered the actual or natural proportions of the bird.

I had some large dry pieces of lime from Wessex Timber (perhaps the tidiest timber yard in the world). I thought lime would suit the subject as it does not look so heavy that flight would seem impossible, and the light colour throws shadows well. By the time I start I have the shape I'm after held firmly in my mind. The question is, will I be able to find it in the wood?

Shape and detail

When I set to with gouge and mallet I feel a rush of impatience. But the potency of woodcarving comes from the slow emergence of a shape that is gradually refined, so I have to settle down. It requires patience and

Michael Henderson was born in Scotland, the son of an engineer. He studied architecture and worked in several countries, including Indonesia. There he was influenced by their view of sculpture as something both spiritual and functional. He moved to Bristol in 1983 to concentrate on woodcarving, and his work is now exhibited and sold widely. He describes his approach as having a 'Scottish engineering foundation with an Oriental super-structure'

There as an interesting asymmetry about the pose

to an exact preconceived outline when starting. This may be quicker, but may also squander a chance to emphasise or distort to good effect as the shape develops.

As you work, think what detail you want to include. Again, balance is important, here between plain forms and detail. Plain forms emphasise the sculptural quality and the wood; detail gives the living presence of the bird. Don't put in detail too soon, in case, for example, an eye is slightly in the wrong place.

This takes a long time — I use almost medieval methods. However, there is a benefit. All the time spent concentrating allows you to identify with the bird and the wood. The pose is refined; the wood is known; ideally artist, wood and bird become one. Paradoxically, because wood is a difficult material to work with, the very effort may draw from us more potent forms.

Rough and smooth

Pieces may be finished smooth or with gouge marks, or a combination of both. A smooth finish shows the wood at its best; the tooled finish shows more of the making process. A smooth finish

is easier to ally with detail, though care must be taken not to lose detail when sanding.

I finished the pelican smooth to bring out the subtle grain lines of the lime. I use progressively finer grades of paper and by the end of a large job my fingerprints are worn away. (I could get a second job as a burglar.) After the finest sanding,

damp the wood to raise the grain. Let it dry and sand again — this gives a gorgeous finish.

The pelican had a coat of Danish oil to seal the wood, a light sand and then wax. With application of the oil comes the moment of judgment: the form is seen for the first time with the colour and grain of the wood. I

A woodcarving has two elements
that must be in balance – the beauty
of the wood and the form

felt the skewed pose had worked well, and the large feathers were nearly powerful enough.

I had wondered all along whether I could use some colour to increase the depth of these feathers or hint at the texture of the bill sack. Now I hesitated. Paint's opacity can distract from the depth of wood by keeping the eye on the surface. I didn't paint.

I was slightly disappointed that my interpretation was more naturalistic and less mythic or heraldic than the pelican and its reputation deserve. But my way is to work strictly from Nature, and that is where my energy comes from. Perhaps in the future Nature will allow me to transform her more. ■

Fine sanding followed by a coat of Danish oil and wax brings out the colour and grain of the lime

TAKING FLIGHT

David Patrick-Brown is a relative newcomer to bird carving, but has become one of its finest exponents. Ken Beynon reports

D avid came to bird carving by a roundabout route. 'I was idling away,' he told me, 'at the Art in Action show at Waterperry near Oxford in 1987, when I came across a stand full of carved ducks and geese. As my wife likes Canada geese I edged in for a closer look. The carver was Bob Ridges and although I liked what I saw I could not afford the prices then, although by today's standards they were not expensive.

'The following year Bob Ridges was not there but another carver was – Judith Nicoll. The mallard drake on her stand stunned me on two counts - its realism and its price! At that time, like so many other people, I did not really value artists' time or skill particularly highly, an attitude I have since altered drastically.

'Judith's comments and carvings convinced me that I should try my hand so, after buying a book of patterns by Anthony Hillman, I carved my first bird. This was a pintail drake. I still have that bird, which is really awful, just to remind me that nothing is ever quite as easy as it seems.' David did not carve another duck until 1990.

Cars and boats

By profession David was an industrial pattern and model maker for companies including McLaren International (making wind tunnel models of their racing cars), Ford, Aston Martin and Jaguar.

Much of his time in the two years before August 1990 were spent making a model of HMS Victory for a client. Made to a scale of ⅛in to a foot, it had thousands of hand-made copper pins in the fully-planked hull and thousands of tiny knots in the rigging. When it

A range of work by
David Patrick-Brown

had been delivered, David's thoughts turned once again to ducks. He spent the next few months teaching himself to carve to an acceptable standard, culminating in his first commission in April 1991. He has been carving full time ever since.

First prizes

David's first entry into a British Decoy and Wildfowl Carvers Association competition was at Slimbridge in June 1991, in his early days as a carver. Despite this, he won first prize at Intermediate level and was widely tipped as a future winner at Open level. This proved to be so: in 1992 he took first prize at Open level with his miniature kingfishers, and two first prizes the following year.

He spends a considerable time studying his subjects, both from life and the specimens

David Patrick-Brown

Carved and painted avocet

at the former Rothschild Zoological Museum at Tring in Hertfordshire. In 1992, with three other woodcarvers, he was invited to exhibit at the museum.

Work and learn

Most of David's commissions now come from the craft fairs he attends each year. 'Carving birds has never been my hobby,' he says. 'So I have had to try and improve while working on clients' carvings. This may sound like having my cake and eating it, but it does have its drawbacks, especially if a new and unpractised

---

Carving birds has never been my hobby, so I have had to try and improve while working

---

technique proves more difficult than anticipated.

'Sometimes a new method will work well and result in better detail or more realistic colouring, but almost always it takes more time – time which has not been allowed for when pricing the carving. Such is the price of progress.'

Material decisions

David carves his waterline birds in jelutong, and other carvings in English lime, although he is increasingly using boxwood for the feet of standing birds and for very small works. The jelutong comes from Timbmet in Oxford. He comments: 'I phone before I go and then I can usually select planks with a general absence of latex holes. However the holes can be useful because the angle through the plank is a good guide to whether it is crown-cut or quarter-sawn. I prefer crown-cut as it makes for easier carving. It comes, of course, from the centre of the log and it seems to take detail better.

'Lime is really the king of the woods for me and is a beautiful wood to carve. I have tried tupelo and didn't get on with it. Perhaps I had a bad piece.

'I use simple tools – a couple of salmon bend chisels, a Swann Morton knife in a brass handle, a set of very old small Marples carving chisels and a 5in Knotts drawknife. I have used a Gesswein power carver for a few months now and find that it is useful in certain situations, but it's not the wonder tool I expected it to be. This may be a reflection of the way I am using it rather than any lack of quality in the tool.'

American perspective

In 1993 David visited the Ward World Bird Carving Championships in Ocean City, Maryland, and gained an insight into the American carving scene.

'I tacked a few days on the end of the first real holiday in years and took a small carving of a kingfisher along, just to show willing and not really knowing what to expect. It was a very sobering experience. The sheer range and depth of skills was almost overwhelming. My little carving sank without trace! I came away resolving to do better but to try to develop my own style further rather than following in American footsteps.'

Demand for his carvings has forced hobbies such as following motor racing and hot-air ballooning onto the back burner. His watercolour painting has been replaced by acrylic painting of his carvings, but he does go birdwatching and plans to do more as part of his efforts to improve the range and quality of his work. 'It may be a truism, but it doesn't matter how good you think you are, there is always someone better. The drive is ever onward and upward and long may it so continue. My wife, unfortunately, is still waiting for her Canada goose.' ■

JIM SPRANKLE
CHAMPION CARVER

JUDITH NICOLL

Judith started carving in 1986 on a week's course run by the late Bob Ridges. Her main occupations then were golf, tennis and embroidery. Now her only activity/occupation is carving almost obsessively.

During her real working life she has been a secretary, a school teacher and, after studying at London University for her MA and Doctorate, an educational researcher.

Her more advanced training in carving was in America with world champion Jim Sprankle. She has exhibited over there at the prestigious Easton Waterfowl Festival, Maryland, and tries to visit each year for courses or shows. Her ambition is to improve her detailed carvings and to learn to paint them in oils.

Her work is in several styles as there is no type of bird carving that does not interest her. She has moved on this last year to carving birds of prey and songbirds.

She puts her progress down to natural doggedness, hard work and the helpfulness of every other carver she knows.

Jim Sprankle has won more awards for his duck sculptures than just about any other carver, including 72 firsts at the World Championships. Here a former student profiles the man and his work.

Scolding widgeon from 1987

Jim Sprankle has been a successful professional pitcher for the Brooklyn Dodgers and the Cincinnati Reds baseball teams, a PR banking executive and a self-employed businessman in refrigeration.

Now, with his wife Patty and son, he lives on the Eastern shore of Maryland, USA. His property, fronting on to the Chesapeake Bay, is on the flight path of many migratory birds, but he does not now, as in his youth, spend his time hunting them. He is a full-time and obsessive professional carver of waterfowl.

Outside his workshop is an aviary for the most important things of all — his reference material. Also there is a large

Jim Sprankle playing for the Cincinnati Reds baseball team in 1960

classroom of the Greenwing University where hundreds of students from Japan to Scotland have gained his certificates with pride. He travels the world to teach with genuine enthusiasm.

His carvings also travel the world and are in both private and public collections. In November Jim was one of the first group of carvers to be admitted to the Waterfowl Festival's National Hall of Fame. This honour specifically recognises individuals who have made outstanding and significant contributions to waterfowl art and conservation efforts on both a national and international level.

Says Jim: "For the first 29 years of my life I dreamed of maybe getting into Baseball's Hall of Fame — but now that I have been chosen as one of the original inductees to the Wildfowl Festival's Hall of Fame I can't imagine being happier or prouder."

Jim's carvings have won him more blue ribbons in competition than probably any other bird carver. He has taken over 72 first place awards at the World Championships. In the major competitions in the United States there are four levels: novice, intermediate, professional and world championship. Jim is a world champion.

This year three of his pieces were chosen for the World Fair in Genoa. Two others are on a tour in Japan, and his work has been chosen for the collections of the most prestigious galleries in the USA.

Yet, he is one of the most down-to-earth, unassuming people you could hope to meet. He is totally approachable, helpful and with an infectious enthusiasm for his art. People faced with such amazingly skilful work can often feel too intimidated to speak to the artist. Jim is a carver for other carvers to meet: he is a top-knotch teacher who believes in sharing. He is also obsessively hard-working and competitive.

My first impression of Jim was made before meeting him. On my first pilgrimage to Easton, that Mecca of birdcarvers' festivals, my husband treated me to a lunch at the famous Tidewater Inn.

In a cabinet running the length of the dining-room was an exhibition of carved ducks. At one end they were breathtakingly realistic and at the other — well, one could say slightly amateur. They were all Jim's.

Two years later, as the featured carver for the Easton Festival's 20th Anniversary, Jim's exhibition stand similarly comprised of a bird from every year, minus one, of his carving career. I now believe he is the only carver to have the confidence and sense of encouragement to show his early work and development so publicly and it exemplifies the man.

Startled sprig pintail from 1989

Red river rockets, greenwing teal from 1990

Mixed flight teal from 1991

At my request he has sent a photograph of a 1972 Bluebill Drake to illustrate this article. He has entitled it *There's always hope!*

Commonsense

Bird carving has reached giddy heights of realism and popularity for collectors as well as carvers in the USA. There are thousands of bird carvers. To succeed at the top level is more than tough.

To become a master carver you have to be able to create pleasing design and graceful form; to capture the character or jizz of the bird; to manage the painstaking detail of soft plumage and rugged flight feathers and, finally, to paint it in such a way as to enhance the accuracy and realism.

Jim has achieved this with his own recognisable and inimitable style. Throughout our conversation I kept pressing him to enunciate the principles and philosophies necessary to make the difference between a good carver and a great one, but all I got were phrases such as 'commitment', 'self-discipline', 'what I like' and 'fun'. There were no grand theories. He loves what he does and he only carves what he wants to carve.

"I know nothing of design. I have never had one art class in my life. As I tell people, I don't even know how to read a colour wheel", he says.

"But, I do use commonsense. When some carvers are questioned about the composition and planning of their piece, I sometimes hear some very sophisticated answers with embellishments of how you do this and that. To me, if the birds in flight look well and look good, then that's the only thing I can go on."

> 'I know nothing of design. I have never had one art class in my life. I don't even know how to read a colour wheel.'

He is not trying to convey any artistic concepts, just "what looks good to me and what I enjoy". However his simple explanations belie the actual ingenuity of what he does.

Carve what interests you

Ducks were always Jim's interest ever since he was a boy growing up on a farm in Indiana where hunting was the main form of recreation. He was a licensed taxidermist by the time he was 16 but, even then, was only interested in working on ducks.

Ducks always intrigued him and when questioned about his ideas and plans for future pieces he admits to referring back to this experience. He spent more hours than he would readily like to admit out hunting and watching bird behaviour.

He is a total specialist, not only through his interest in ducks, but because he believes that to carve well and to be well-known for it, you must focus in on something. To be successful you need to "pick something and learn it and do it well".

As you get older your skills do not improve but "being able to read reference material and being able to transfer what you see through your hands onto a carving, that's what makes your carvings get better as you get older or progress in your carving."

He advises every carver to keep their mind open and experiment: never think in terms of how quickly you can carve something and sell it. Never forget your name is on the bottom. But overall he says that good carving comes from what you are personally interested in. You're going to do it better.

Beginnings and the future

Jim's first carvings were a rig of ten cork decoys to hunt over about 25 years ago. He

still owns one but gave the rest away. His first wooden carving was a Goldeneye pair which were flat bottomed and "I thought were decorative birds". By this he means highly detailed birds termed 'decorative' in competition.

He never dreamed he would have a future career carving detailed birds and that after 1972 he would never think of doing anything else, or that he would be thinking in terms of wanting to be known as one of the best duck carvers of his day.

In those days hunting took priority. Now he goes to Arkansas only once a year to hunt with friends who also invite Bill Clinton. Perhaps Jim's next piece will be featured in the White House!

Pintails over the Choptank river, from 1992

For Jim the ideal existence would be to have the freedom to have as many days in his workshop carving as possible. With all his teaching he finds it difficult to have what he calls quality time for carving. He is teaching in the South one weekend, Canada the next and maybe the UK the next.

He admits to having certain nebulous plans for carving some really special pieces just for him to keep. But practicality and the demands of financial security prevent this at present. Most artists have these future ideas floating about and Jim recognises that his

last two flying Teal pieces are "a sort of mini of what I want to do".

The piece he was working on for the Spring World Championship had three Teal ducks flying over March grass. "I would like to do five or seven Teal dusting across this grass, diving out of the sky or something.

"There are lots of things that I would like to do but times are changing and most all of us cannot get by on just carving. That's why you find some of us teaching and writing books — how many years away it is before I can just carve for myself I don't know."

For some of us, carving full-time professionally kills the enjoyment. Jim's talk, however, is still full of the excitement of carving even after 25 years. "I feel just as excited each morning when I get into my workshop, knowing what I'm going to do and what I'm trying to accomplish." Really the future for Jim consists of having as many days in his workshop carving as possible.

Pintail drake from 1985

Competitions

There were some years when Jim did not enter his birds in competitions and he admits that these were some of the most enjoyable times when he was suiting himself, stretching his imagination. He believes that those pieces were the best engineered, the best worked and the most creative.

"Competition curtails creativity, I don't think there is any question about it." But, and here he gives a big but, it helps the carver evaluate his work. Winning keeps you wanting to do better, and if you want recognition there is no quicker way.

He remembers the thrill of the first Best in Show rosette, but warns of the danger of reaching the stage where the carver might put winning before anything else — or the thrill of not losing!

He also became disillusioned with the collectors' obsession with buying only birds with blue ribbons. He remembers taking eight birds to a competition and all were sold unseen before the judging took place. Seven took blue first place rosettes but a collector returned the one that only took second place. Jim would rather burn a bird than sell another to that man.

Red River Rockets had been a special piece for Jim, breaking new ground in both the design and the choice of a base of heated glass. He is keen to do new things and he prides himself in having new ideas in design and composition. He decided only two weeks before the Championships to enter the piece. He really didn't want someone else copying it and getting the credit for it before himself. He wanted people to see it and there was no better place.

A bluebill drake carved by Jim in 1972 entitled There's Always Hope!

Teaching and sharing

Of course carvers will copy others' work. "Of course we all copy to a degree the things we like and esteem." Jim's birds and style are copied now all over the world but he likes to think his students develop into their own style.

The Americans are famous for their friendliness and hospitality. This extends into extreme helpfulness in the carving world and then more some from Jim. As a student of his, I found there was no question he did not consider carefully and answer fully.

He loves to teach in the UK. He loves the way we do not interrupt his demos but save our questions for the end, listening to him and each other so courteously! He finds teaching as rewarding as winning. It has added another dimension to the carving world — he has gained so many friends and learned so much from his students.

"Before I used to just sit year after year and crank out carvings, and now I look forward to my classes." Many students here will agree on the value and fun of classes with Jim.

It is important for all carvers to share what they know. Jim talks of the carvers who helped him and points out that until another carver knows what you know he is not able to help you. "If you share what you know with the other carvers in the community, you subconsciously try harder to keep ahead of these folks."

'Competition curtails creativity, I don't think there is any question about it. But it helps the carver evaluate his work.'

He thinks it is only the insecure who don't want to help others. He credits carvers in the USA with being quick to help beginners but the information dries a little as they become very good. Some of the best are slow to actually praise novices and tell them they are doing good work.

Encouragement is the basis of Jim's teaching. We all have creativity in us and sometimes it just takes someone to encourage you. With all the books, tapes, magazines and courses available today for the beginner, all it takes is commitment. "You have to make sacrifices and focus on carving and work at it with a self-discipline."

Commissions

Jim talks as a professional and thinks constantly in terms of selling his work. "In art, as in anything else, you have to sell your product. Whether we understand, believe or realise it, we're selling every minute our eyes are open."

He sees most of the different occupations of his working life as bound up with selling. You have to sell yourself first to sell a carving. But selling in advance has its problems.

He advises beginners not to take on too many commissions because they are worried about security, and certainly never to take a down payment and be hounded to death by the purchaser. He finds most collectors do not specify how they want the bird — only the species. Commissions can inhibit the artist but sales are important.

Woodcarving and art

As with so many of us in the carving world, Jim is disappointed in the boundaries of the art world. He speaks of a time when on a trip to New York he saw some modern sculpture in a gallery with price tags of thousands and felt some anger in himself that this was called art and what he does is not.

However he is resigned to his 'gripe' as there is nothing he can do about it. The gallery people are the ones who dictate what is art. He does not think that most people have the concept of what the decorative floating carving really is.

Here we had a little discussion over my British use of the word 'carvings'. 'Sculpture' is the word he prefers, believing that to call a piece a 'carving' denotes craft. Carving to him is someone doing floating birds and hunting over them. He tries to get his flying birds away from the craft habitat scene of being hung on tree branches.

He is trying to clean up his pieces and make them more simplistic. "You just have to carve what you like and hope that that is good enough". There are changes in the extreme realism demanded by competition, and certainly competition rosettes can define a carver's financial security.

For Jim the plumage and realism is important and he will do it anyway. But artists are being allowed looser and more interpretative work in the competition environment. Galleries are accepting woodcarvings and appropriating money to buy for their collections.

Finally I asked him if there was any one bird with which he was satisfied. A definite answer came back that the day you see the carving you are satisfied with that will be the best carving you ever do.

Complacency can come if you listen to people raving about your work, and they will do if they have nothing else to compare it to. Every piece prompts him to try harder with the next one. ∎

SMALL BUT PERFECT

Vic Wood describes the exquisite work of Australian netsuke carver Susan Wraight

A former jeweller, Susan Wraight is one of only 50 people in the world practising the ancient Japanese art of netsuke carving. These tiny exquisite objects were used originally over a period of three centuries as toggles for suspending small boxes, for snuff or medicine, from the kimono. Silk cords threaded through holes linked the netsuke to an inro, a box about 2in, 50mm long, and an ojime, a slider used to hold the inro closed.

Netsuke have many of the qualities of jewellery: they are portable, beautifully made, designed to be handled by the wearer and are a wonderful vehicle for self-expression.

They are in great demand and fetch high prices from international collectors. This year alone Susan's work will be exhibited in South America, Edinburgh, London, Los Angeles and Tokyo. The pieces are so fine that she only makes 20 in a year.

One notable work, a tiny platypus measuring only 40mm, 1½in long, was for former US President George Bush. It was commissioned by the government of Victoria as the state's official gift to the President during his visit to Australia in 1992.

Susan's pieces are the result of meticulous observation. She gives a wide berth to the sentimental 'fluffy bunny' approach to nature. 'Netsuke can, if you're not careful, become cutesy. I abhor cutesiness. I strive to get an unsentimental view of nature.' Equally, however, she avoids the tendency in some antique netsuke towards the macabre and grotesque. Rather, she says, her work is a joyful celebration of the natural world.

She describes her initial reaction to antique netsuke as one of fascination. 'They are functional objects, but also works of sculpture, and although made in non-precious materials, such as wood or ivory, they have a precious quality about them. There is great skill in their making and marvellous attention to detail.

'Work on such a small scale allows an intimate interaction between the owner and the

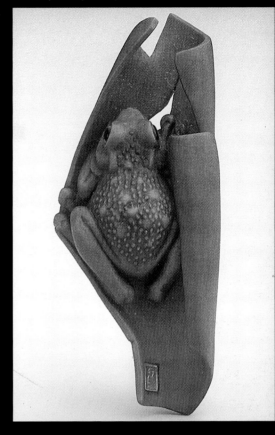

Netsuke can, if you're not careful, become cutesy. I abhor cutesiness. I strive to get an unsentimental view of nature

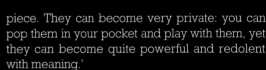

Possum's Nest, part of the 'things hidden' series, encourages the onlooker to handle the piece to discover its full meaning

piece. They can become very private: you can pop them in your pocket and play with them, yet they can become quite powerful and redolent with meaning.'

Susan is currently working on three different series of netsuke, one of which has 'things hidden' as the central aspect of the design. *Possum's Nest* and *Frog in Bark* are both typical examples.

'While looking at my work one day, I realised that my netsuke were very accessible,' she says. 'As intended, the carvings were generally easily read and understood, but I wondered if perhaps they revealed themselves a little too quickly.

'I embarked upon a series of carvings that revolved around the theme of things hidden, wherein the subject is partially screened from the onlooker. I wanted to slow the process of perception – to create an element of ambiguity that would entice the onlooker to be curious about the netsuke and pick it up, explore it, turning it over and over until finally the secret of

Gibbons,
one of a series
showing creatures
intertwined

its nature and identity would be revealed.'

Gibbons and *Fighting Flight* are part of another series exploring the possibilities of designs showing creatures entwined. They generate pattern, rhythm and movement as they interact with one another, telling stories of their own.

Susan hopes they also invite the onlooker to provide a narrative that contributes to the life of the netsuke and creates an intimacy between it and the viewer.

The third series is represented here by *The Lion and the Mouse*, a set of netsuke and ojime. As Susan explains, 'It depicts one of Aesop's fables. In the sixth century BC a Greek slave named Aesop wrote a set of short pithy stories, full of concentrated energy, that showed life as it was, not as it might have been. His fables are as relevant now as they were then, and they seem to me to be an ideal subject for netsuke - the two disparate disciplines having many parallels, not least being a significance out of all proportion to size.' ■

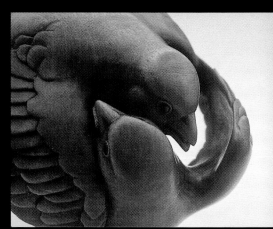

Vic Wood has been among the top names in Australian woodworking for more than 15 years, and is established as a teacher, lecturer and writer. He originally trained in gold and silver-smithing, and now his turned and carved work is represented in collections throughout the world

Fighting Flight – the two birds generate pattern, rhythm and movement

Derek George with an eagle he carved for the Alliance and Leicester Building Society

AS GOOD AS GOLD

HUGH GRAHAM

Derek George has come to the conclusion that carvings can be as precious as the work of gold or silversmiths, admirers of his workmanship agree.

Walking through the New Forest with Derek George is a trial of patience — every fallen piece of timber is examined in case it contains a carving. Four hours later, and with dusk spreading through the sky, we get back to his car, looking like foresters bringing kindling home for the fire.

Derek looks at wood in a different way to the rest of us. He's a wild life carver, using wood's natural characteristics to suggest the fine detail of the creatures he immortalises: 'When I look at wood I study the grain, annual rings and medullary rays. London plane, for example, has very distinctive ray patterns — depending upon

Derek was given this piece some time ago. He thinks it is an African hardwood. One day he's going to carve an otter emerging from the centre of the distinctive swirls

the size of the trunk or bough — and these can be carved to represent a bird that's speckled; perhaps a thrush or a pheasant in flight.

'I've got a strange piece here. I've no idea what it is — an African hardwood I think, given to me by a customer about ten years ago. But look at the swirl. Eventually I'll have an otter coming out of the centre of those rings. Beautiful!'

He pauses to pick up a half carved kingfisher. 'I'm making this out of laburnum — a beautiful wood, much prized by carvers. It's not commercial, so most firms can't be bothered to store it for ten years, but the one or two that do would have charged £20.00 for the small log this came from, and because of the way I work, I've thrown three quarters of it away! And Laburnum is not expensive — African blackwood (*Dalbergia melanoxylon*) is more than £400.00 a cubic foot!

'It's not until customers consider the cost of wood, which most people think of as cheap until they put up a shelf, that one can begin to debate the true value of a woodcarving.' He's clearly off on a favourite subject. 'Woodcarvings can be as precious in many ways as work produced by gold and silversmiths. The value is in the design and the skill of the craftsman. 'He pauses to pick up an exquisite bluetit, 'I've been carving bluetits for 20 years, but I've only once been able to produce a sculpture with markings exactly like the real thing — the little topknot, the black bit that runs through the eyes.' He caresses the carving, 'I'd never sell this piece. It's unique. Absolutely priceless.'

He turns to put the bluetit down and picks up a snake. 'Look at this, it's carved from turu palm (*Caryota urens* or palmwood I think, Ed.). The tree consists of black, carbon-like, rods running up the trunk, surrounded by light brown wood. By carving along the length I can produce zig-zag lines on the back, but by working across the rods I create spots along the sides and the belly. 'People find it difficult to believe so many effects can be achieved from one piece of wood.'

The only piece that Derek will never sell. A bluetit carved from laburnum, with every natural marking in the right place

Right
Derek putting the finishing touches to a tern, carved from ash, in his workshop

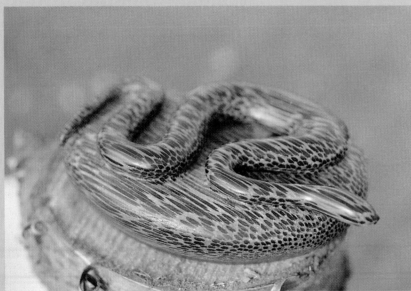

Snake carved from turu palm — notice how by carving along and across the carbon like rods running through the light brown wood, that Derek has managed to create a speckled effect along the creature's belly

Early start

Derek was born in 1931 and lost his father at the beginning of the war. He and his younger brother, Colin, were brought up by their mother and grandfather.

'Grandfather bought me my first pen-knife and taught me how to whittle. I used to sit by his shed cutting away. The results were dreadful, but I got better, making whistles and so on. And that's how it all began really — just whittling away at various woods — I didn't attempt to carve anything properly until 1970, but I always had a knife in my pocket.

'At school, even though I was a dunce, I managed to win a scholarship to Art School. I couldn't take it, though, because Mum was bringing us up on her own and we couldn't afford the money. So I became apprenticed to a tailor, which didn't suit me at all.' He grins at his little joke. 'After making suits for six years I left the rag trade, but nothing learned is ever wasted, because my nimble fingers were to prove useful later.

'I wanted to work in the country, not easy in Hounslow, so I did the next best thing and became a groundsman. During the cricket season I had to patch and roll the wicket between innings, so to fill in the time I sat on the boundary whittling away. I can remember an old chair leg becoming a crocodile; terribly crude, but it was a start — and I still have it.'

Country craft

Derek had always hankered after the country life, and his chance came in 1970 when he moved to Stubbington, Hampshire, setting up as a landscape gardener. Derek found in carving the creative fulfilment denied him as a teenager. Better still, paring shavings helped him to relax from the pressures of running his business. He gave most of his early attempts away, but as word of his skill spread through Hampshire he began to receive commissions. Within three years his hobby was generating a useful supplementary income, which was just as well because in 1976 he damaged his lower back so badly he was told he'd never work in landscape gardening again.

It was Pamela, his wife, who suggested he become a woodcarver to support their family of three children. At that time he'd three dozen unsold carvings. 'Nothing

The same tern, but free-standing, beautifully worked

ventured, nothing gained,' is Derek's motto, so he talked the Harrods craft buyer into looking at his work. He was very impressed and took the lot! Wonderful! But six months later Harrods had not paid him for the 12 pieces they'd sold. They paid up eventually, but Derek decided it was nonsense for him to finance Harrods, so he removed the remaining pieces and ever since has sold his work through small galleries and direct commissions.

'The one good thing to come out of the Harrods experiment was that Lord Dulverton, of the Wills tobacco family, bought a little nuthatch. One morning he phoned to say one of his staff had broken the beak. I replaced it and he became a great patron.'

Derek's woodstore —most of it is either found in the woods, or given to him by friends who scavenge woodlands for him. A large number of pieces are given by patrons

Derek erected a shed at the bottom of his garden, and turned it into a workshop. 'From the beginning I could see the shapes of birds and other creatures in woodgrain. Sometimes I might see a dolphin or an otter. It was very exciting.'

His first efforts fetched around £25.00 each, and since he was able to produce six a month, managed to carve a new career for himself-even though it took five or six days to produce a wren, one of his most popular subjects. Today, providing there are no interruptions, he can finish a wren in two days — 'but it's taken me 20 years to work that quickly'.

He's now made 1,543 carvings, averaging 70 a year, the most recent selling for £300.00, or more, despite the recession. They're tiny, the largest could be shipped in a one cubic foot box, in a variety of woods that are exquisitely worked, but never stained, painted or tinted, only polished.

Craft or art

To begin with, patrons' invoices were his only record. He thought it sufficient to note — Killer Whale in African Blackwood —

the name of the customer and the date of purchase. But all this changed in 1976 at a crafts exhibition. A fellow exhibitor, Ralph Gillies Cole, a well-known watercolour artist, stood on his stand for about half an hour watching Derek respond to potential purchasers. 'He told me I was losing sales because I did not value my own work sufficiently highly. "How long did it take you to carve this?' He asked. 'About a week and a half,' I replied. 'There you are then,' he said triumphantly. 'It's really valuable — an antique in the making. You get a fair price for your carvings now,' he said, 'but think what they are going to be worth in years to come.'

They talked for quite a long while, discussing relative costs. It was agreed that the cost of paintings is not related to the time it takes to paint them and folk know that prices asked by artists can vary between

£25.00 and £25,000. It's a fact that a small watercolour dashed off in a couple of hours can fetch £100.00. It takes Derek two days to earn £100.00 from carving.

'My friend gave me a whole new perspective. I wrote to each of my former customers asking for precise measurements and photographs of the pieces they'd bought. With that information I started a log book. I've now got a detailed description of every sculpture I've carved. Somewhere on each I've burned my autograph **dg** and the date.

'I'm grateful to my patrons because they've made it possible for my family to enjoy a wonderful way of life. My log will make it impossible to fake additional pieces when I'm dead and gone. That way I'm protecting the investments my patrons have made.'

Tools and technique

Derek discovered very early on that penknives, indeed any knives with tapered cross-section blades, are difficult to carve with. 'It's impossible to manoeuvre the blades. Chisels are easier because the bevel can be used to lever away the waste — but the blades are too long.

Above
Derek carves dozens of wrens every year, they are his top seller. Like these examples they are usually carved from elm and mounted on Irish bogwood

Top left
Polishing a blue whale carved from lignum vitae — Derek used 1000 grade wet and dry to finish this piece. 'The wood is so hard,' he says, 'that anything coarser leaves marks almost impossible to remove during the polishing stage'

'So I decided to make my own knives. A friend suggested machine hacksaw blades for the steel. In 1975 they were quite thick, top quality all the way through — not like modern blades, soft metal with hardened teeth!

'Gradually my perfect knife emerged — a long, 5" 125mm handle with a short blade about 1" 25mm in length. By trial and error I devised the sort of handle that fitted my hands comfortably. I also worked out the different blades I needed, particularly those needed to explore tiny crevices. Every so often I had to stop carving to design a blade for a particularly intricate carving. Each new knife was added to the collection.

'It took me about five years to devise my basic kit, and I've just discovered the Japanese are now making knives remarkably like mine. I've bought a set. They're very good, but the blades taper, so I've ground them down to take a bevel and they work fine — not quite as good as my own knives, but I expect that's because I'm used to them.'

Derek's main power tool is a Startrite 352 Bandsaw; with this he cuts sections through the various woods he uses, in order to find the elusive design. Then he outlines the carving in pencil on the wood and cuts the basic profile on the bandsaw, carefully selecting woods which provide colour contrast — he never laminates woods together, to create different tones.

'I've experimented with all sorts of vices, but none have helped me. I hold the workpiece in my hands — sometimes supporting it on a carving post — because I'm constantly turning and shaping. You've got to have strong wrists for this work, and there's no time to be clamping and unclamping the workpiece in the vice.'

Derek also uses these block cutters' tools for his work, his relatively small carvings don't require larger tools

Derek has some Japanese chip carving tools reground to suit his own style of working

Derek does most of his work with these knives he made, the handles are turned from beech, the ferrules are cut from 1/2" 13mm diameter copper pipe, the blades are ground from industrial hacksaw blades

Below
A close view of Derek's knives shows the prominent bevels, and ferrules that have been filed away to prevent them fouling the work

I watched him carving for about five minutes. The blade moved in short, deft strokes, removing almost transparent rice paper thick shavings, about the size of a fly's wing. The tool handle rested across the palm, index finger curled around the top of the haft, braced against the blade, providing great power. Suddenly the grip would be reversed and he'd be cutting away from him. Thirty seconds later he would be holding the knife like a pen, teasing a crevice clear of waste.

Every now and then he'd change knives, always replacing the discarded one carefully in its box before picking up another. His wrists, although slim, are immensely powerful and Derek says he can work non-stop for hours.

'I use a wide range of small files for finishing, prior to sanding with silicon carbide papers, beginning with what I call a coarse paper, 100 grade, gradually reducing to 600 and sometimes 1,000 grade wet and dry. A smooth, highly polished finish is my trademark. When I'm satisfied I polish with *Bri-Wax*.'

He turns up wooden bases on a Coronet lathe; drills holes for the beaks on a Nutool drill press and also uses a Kity combination tool — mainly as a planer and thicknesser.

'I mount each sculpture on Irish bogwood. I bought a load years ago. The rough texture provides a wonderful contrast between the carving and the highly polished base.'

Because Derek enjoys his work so much he's happy to help others improve their skills and for this reason he is prepared to teach carvers on a one-to-one basis in his workshop, and at the courses he runs for up to 12 students at Earnley Concourse. Those interested in individual tuition can contact Derek George at his home, West Lodge, 18 Elizabeth Road, Stubbington, Hampshire PO14 2RF, Telephone: 0329-662458. Details of his Earnley Courses can be obtained from Owain Roberts, The Director, Earnley Concourse, Earnley, near Chichester, West Sussex PO20 7JL. ■

Judith started carving in 1986 on a week's course run by the late Bob Ridges. Her main occupations then were golf, tennis and embroidery. Now her only activity/ occupation is carving almost obsessively.

During her real working life she has been a secretary, a school teacher and, after studying at London University for her MA and Doctorate, an educational researcher.

Her more advanced training in carving was in America with world champion Jim Sprankle. She has exhibited over there at the prestigious Easton Waterfowl Festival, Maryland, and tries to visit each year for courses or shows. Her ambition is to improve her detailed carvings and to learn to paint them in oils.

Her work is in several styles as there is no type of bird carving that does not interest her.

She has moved on this last year to carving birds of prey and songbirds.

She puts her progress down to natural doggedness, hard work and the helpfulness of every other carver she knows.

SWANS BIRDS AND OTHER ANIMALS

Judith Nicoll visited Jim Tooker, Martin Gates and Howard Suzuki, three carvers in Florida with different styles of work.

You are only as good as your reference material. This must have been said to many carvers who wish to improve the standard of their work. Likewise they are instructed to: 'carve what you know and carve what you like.' The results will show! In Florida I was lucky enough to meet three carvers who all follow these precepts and who base their work on the wildlife of their region, but whose styles differ extraordinarily. Let me introduce them to you.

Jim Tooker carves his swans on a manic macro scale with large power tools (we're talking chainsaws here), to relax after a hard day running his businesses.

In stark contrast Martin Gates studies the grain of the wood very carefully before massaging it with one of his collection of over two hundred antique carving tools. His work is deceptively simple but reveals the essence of the animals he has chosen to make his life's study.

Howard Suzuki, on the other hand, is a respected marine biologist who describes his work as aquatic life sculptures, which are entirely based on his professional, academic field work, and diving the oceans of the world.

Jim Tooker

Visiting Jim in his workshop confirms my European image of the typical American: big; courteous; ebullient; enthusiastic and efficient. In his well-organised workshop he had set up everything especially so that he could show me all the different stages of his work. He carves for two hours every night as therapy after heavy days spent running two businesses. He uses a full range of tools, hand and power, as he is not a purist and wants to let the carving out of the wood.

He carves swans and each one takes about twenty hours, although five or six are finished before the painting stage. Jim sticks to swans because he says that they have more poses than other birds: 'a million attitudes.' Also, not many carvers make them as they work out expensive to buy.

The wood used is basswood (*Tilia americana*), or white cedar (*Chamaecyparis thyoides*) which is shipped-in in loads of up to 1000 board feet a time from Pennsylvania or Tennessee. Each swan has about $80 US worth in it. He speaks of willow (*Salix sp.*) being the nicest wood he ever used as he could put so much detail on it.

In the traditional way, the top view is drawn out first direct on to the block of wood. No patterns are used, Jim draws the shapes freestyle from memory. The two blocks for the body are hot-glued together and cut out on the bandsaw. The side profile is then sketched on and bandsawn.

White swans are Jim's speciality

A metal plate is screwed on to the swan's base which in turn fits on to a power arm vice. The arm is banged into place firmly with a hammer before the swan is attacked energetically with a chainsaw. Even Jim's rasp is bigger and more powerful than any I've seen. It is a 'Shinto', Japanese, and looks like it is manufactured out of many hacksaw blades.

The power sander comes next and again the wood flies as Jim attacks with gusto. The swan is then hollowed with the chainsaw: it

Jim Tooker at work on one of his swans

is quicker than a drill press!

Progress, speed and efficiency are what matters to Jim. Carving with hammer and chisel used to take him three days. He now spends about six hours on the body and another six on the head and neck. My overall impression is of a high-powered businessman who still loves to work with his hands.

He has fun with the power of power tools and often refers to the time saved. This does not tell the full story, however, because although he uses modern man's justification that 'it's faster this way' I believe that he uses these machines at least partly for the sheer exuberance of their operation.

Besides relaxation, I asked him, why did he ever start carving? It turned out that his wife had gone on a chair-caning course and so he took a next-door course on carving caricatures just to be sociable. The next year Jim was teaching his teacher! The eventual result was 'antique' decoy swans, in the style of a bygone era, carved in a thoroughly modern way.

Martin Gates

In complete contrast to Jim, Martin Gates carves using only antique tools. He started with a set inherited from his grandfather. Now, has a collection of over two hundred tools, many of which he acquired on trips to Europe, on buying trips for his father's antique shop. Pride in his tools and the feeling of control they give him is what characterises his work.

Although he favours the old tools, because of the quality of their steel, he tells the story of one of his teachers who swore that modern tools, having been buried in mule manure to corrode and then cleaned up, would hold their edge even better. Recently Martin has taken to leaving the tool marks on his work, just lightly sanding over them.

He prizes the natural colour and figure of woods and, although he has been considering having his work cast in bronze, he finds that what people really appreciate is the hand work in his pieces and the feel of the wood.

Probably only eight or nine carvings are completed each year, with a major piece taking several hundred hours and selling for very worthwhile money. All his pieces have a natural finish and he carves them out of one piece, so as not to have any surface marks from glue joints. He likes to read the grain and character of the wood and, to a certain extent, let it dictate the design.

He does not have a pre-conceived definitive pattern and adapts his artistic

Black gold, black death by Martin Gates, from one piece of walnut 29 x 36 x 25in

notion to any difficulties or opportunities discovered in the wood as he progresses. Cherry with its tight grain and consistency, and walnut are his favourites. He enjoys the different colours of walnut created by the

Fishmongers by
Martin Gates,
spalted pecan
34 x 30 x 27in

natural variety of different minerals in
different states. In his yard are huge logs
slowly seasoning.

Martin's inspiration is all from wildlife
— from his boyhood in Oregon, and
particularly from the wading birds of the
area of central Florida in which he now
lives. Here he is presented with the graceful
shape and form of egrets and herons, and
the viewer is made to share their lush, semi-
tropical habitat.

To illustrate how he works, Martin
showed me photographs of the different
stages of a sculpture of a falcon attacking a
duck. As one looks back from the finished
piece to the rough log which spawned it, one
can trace the original image Martin had of

the shapes of the birds trapped in the piece
of wood. He concentrates on his vision-
scene and sees how he can formulate it from
a particular log.

Based on his knowledge of the forms of
the wildlife, and their anatomy, he can
determine which stance will produce the
image and expression he wants. It is better
to have a clear picture of the finished piece
before starting. He wants his work dramatic
and realistic but artistically pleasing to the
viewer. However, as he gets into the logs he
can meet trouble spots. He may have to
change his original concept — or even the
species of a duck — where after roughing
out any rotten part, the wood will not
accommodate his ideas.

Shadow stalker by
Martin Gates, holly
7 x 4 x 3½in

Egret and Turtle
by **Martin Gates**,
cherry
27 x 16 x 12in

Sea turtle by
Martin Gates,
cherry 14 x 8 x 4in

Once he has rough-cut the main block, he strategically places heavy paper silhouette patterns on to it and pencils around them. He then moves around the piece with gouges, rasps and chisels removing wood how he can. His large pieces do not fit on to a movable power arm vice.

Martin started woodcarving as a boy using his grandfather's tools, but has had no formal art training. He has strengthened his technical background working on repairs and restoration of antiques in his father's shop, but also found himself influenced by the high quality woods and craftsmanship of the mouldings and figures he had to replace on the European antiques. His interest in carving birds started after seeing carved miniatures at an art show whilst on a buying trip.

He took two months as an apprentice to the artist, Dan DeMendoza. Once back home in the family business he carved some birds and took some time with a specialist animal woodcarver, Jack Hall, who taught him the basics of traditional woodcarving.

Sometimes people have to wait until retirement before they can find the time to fully develop an interest; sometimes circumstances conspire to catapult them into it. In Martin's case it was a particularly disturbing burglary in the antique shop which convinced him not to wait to do what he really wished, and dedicate himself to something that was important to him.

In 1987, therefore, Martin put a piece into his first competition and won first place in the World Class Championship, Natural Finish Lifesize division. In less than three years he proceeded to win most of the prestigious prizes for his style category in the USA, and had been invited to exhibit at the most important shows. He is now a full-time professional whose family depends on his success. But, Martin is still first and foremost a visionary artist. His pleasure in his work shines through, and he can use his art to useful purpose to constantly promote a love and concern for wildlife.

How many artists would dare to carve a disturbing piece on death after reading about the Exxon Valdez oil spill? 'The female eagle is crying in pain and sorrow for what we've done to the world — ours and hers.'

He used a propane torch on the base and skull to create the effect of oil on a beach.

Martin's success does not just come from his craftsmanship and the artistry of his lines, but from his ability to communicate his knowledge and love of nature to a people who are rendered increasingly remote from it by the constraints of urban life.

Howard Suzuki

Howard is a dedicated admirer of the animals of the waters of Florida. He is a marine biologist and supremely qualified to carve the subtle differences which distinguish, for instance, the different species of whales. A quiet, modest and professional man, he describes his carving as 'stylised realism' for it emphasises shape and form artistically, but is anatomically correct. He uses the natural grain and colour of wood in his planning and never enhances with stain.

I was fascinated as he introduced me to the subjects of his carvings on show at the Charleston Exposition: Florida 'gators, humpback whales and sailfish. Where other carvers may observe their subject birds with binoculars, Howard dives to mingle with his marine animals and has years of academic study and research behind him. After my return to the UK he sent me some slides and full descriptions of the sculptures. I decided to let him speak for himself as his words communicate far better than I can the exacting care with which he approaches his carving.

Anhinga by
Howard Suzuki,
Sweetbay
magnolia
17 x 10 x 10in

▌▌ My Anhinga is made out of Sweetbay magnolia (*Magnolia virginiana*). The fish is part of the woodblock and was naturally dark brown. The dark wood was a portion of the tree that was, apparently, struck by lightning; the dark wood formed as part of the healing process. The dark wood is seen extending into the base just behind the anhinga's neck. A small piece of light coloured wood can be seen on the gill cover.

Anhingas spear their prey, although normally not this deep into the beak. The amount of available wood, both dark and light, determined size and location of the fish on the bird's beak, its size and shape. The thinness of the black portion determined that I could not carve a round-bodied fish such as a minnow, but was limited to carve a laterally compressed fish such as a centrarchid sunfish. **▌▌**

I had this piece of wood for about five years, not knowing what I could make out of it. One day the idea came all of a sudden. I then made all kinds of measurements to determine as closely as possible where the black portion would be located at each depth. This was like a crude radiologic tomography, without sophisticated instrumentation. I finally concluded that I had to make it 80% lifesize to maximise the use of the wood. And I guessed correctly! It measures 17 x 10 x 10in.

Mother alligator and hatchlings This is carved in pecan wood (*Carya illinoensis*) and is a life-size sculpture of a head of a 9½ft 'gator with its 9in hatchlings. The mother is protecting its newly hatched progeny, particularly from the hungry bull 'gators. The hatchlings enjoy resting on the mother's head. This sculpture is the result of some six years' field work assisting the Florida Freshwater Game and Fish Commission and the US Fish and Wildlife Service in their co-operative alligator research project during part of each summer. 42 x 18 x 8in.

Mother alligator and hatchlings by Howard Suzuki, pecan wood 42 x 18 x 8in

Flamingos by Howard Suzuki, buttonwood mangrove 17 x 15 x 12in

Flamingos Carved in buttonwood mangrove (*Laguncularia racemosa*) commonly found along the tidal flats in Florida and the Caribbean. Whilst an International Exchange Artist in the Netherlands Antilles, I was inspired to carve a flamingo. Bonaire has about 15,000 flamingos, so I had ample opportunities to observe and photograph them in their natural habitat. After returning, I examined and photographed 'skins' in the Florida Natural History Museum. I chose an unusual piece of buttonwood I had purchased in the Florida Keys some five or six years ago. Suddenly the design crystallised. The natural curvature of the wood finally formulated the design. Full size head and neck 15 x 12 x 17in walnut base.

Unsuspecting by Howard Suzuki, black walnut 18 x 10 x 3in

Unsuspecting This is an American alligator silently swimming towards an unsuspecting swimming duck. Made in American black walnut (*Juglans nigra*) which was sawn from the tree at an angle. Not all slabs are suitable for this particular design as the pattern of the wood grain determines whether or not the wood meets the design criteria, and the location of the duck and shape of the alligator. The waves are coordinated with the pattern of the grain. The pessimist concludes that the duck will be taken, while the optimist feels that the duck will get away. I leave the conclusion to the viewer. 18 x 10 x 3in. ∎

CARVING KEEPS ME YOUNG

JOHN E. PAYNE

The gentleman unpacked a set of old hunting figures from a tin box and set them out on my table. "Now there's some carving for you," he said. "You won't believe this," I said, "but I carved those pieces myself about 50 years ago."

Hunters and pack in 'full cry' after fox

I started woodcarving some 70 years ago, using my pocket-knife to whittle strange faces, animals and snakes from the roots and growths I found along the rocky banks of the river, and many burns, on the North Country Estate where I spent my childhood.

At about the age of 12, I joined the Boy Scout movement and continued my carving, using a small hand axe. With this I fashioned totem poles and decorated them by burning with a red-hot iron and bright oil paints.

Carved pintail decoy

Carved curlew (commission)

Carved scaup decoy

The totems were sold for Scout funds and I got orders from other troops of Scouts in the area. At that time, I received a commission to carve a walking-stick for Baden Powell. This was presented to him at the Northern Counties Jamboree in 1936. I also carved a walking-stick for the famous clown 'Coco' who was with Bertram Mills Circus.

During the same period, I also carved duck and pigeon decoys for the game keepers and shooting folk in the area. For these I used branches of ash wood, shaped so that I could get the bodies and heads out of one piece. My tools at the time were a hand axe, a heavy blacksmith's rasp and a 2" 50mm straight chisel.

It was not until 1980 that I started carving decoys again. I was able to buy in a good stock of yellow pine from a second-hand timber dealer. Huge beams of yellow pine had been used in the building of Lancashire cotton mills. As many of these were demolished at that time, the timber came on to the market.

Decoys

I had the beams sawn into blocks, 5" x 6" 125mm x 150mm square and 40" 1015mm long. I am able to get three various kinds of duck from each block.

For the marking out of the duck shapes, I use plywood templates made from my own drawings. With a Victorian butcher's cleaver, I hack out the duck shapes. These are then finished, using 'Surform' slim line knives and assorted grades of 'Scotch' sandpaper. I have found nothing to compare with them over the years.

Many of my clients prefer carvings in natural woods, so that the grain, colour and toolmarks can be appreciated. For these, in addition to the yellow pine, I use oak, ash, elm, cherry and spalted sycamore. With careful planning, the spalted marks will show up like feathering on both sides of the finished bird.

I make my own polish, using four ounces of pure beeswax to half a pint of pure turpentine. I heat the ingredients until the solution looks like cream. It is used cold. The final buffing with a clean pad of linen or woollen material brings out a lovely lasting shine, which in turn brings out the grain and colours of the natural wood.

Painting

For the painting of birds and decoys, after sealing with a primer, I use 'acrylic' paints. There are many bird magazines and books available

from which good coloured photographs and prints can be obtained. I firebrand all my larger carvings with my initials, using a branding iron made by a friend.

From the age of 17, until I was about 22, I was able to earn my living with my carvings. I carved many family crests, and coats of arms, during this time.

Unbreakable

I had been given the carving of a spaniel dog. I found, on examination, that it had been constructed with sawn-out sections, and then glued together, so that the woodgrain ran along the body, legs and tail of the dog. This method assured that none of the pieces were cut with a short grain. Thus, when finished, they were very strong and almost unbreakable.

Using this method, I carved figures of country folk, farm animals and every breed of dog. I used a proportion of 1" 25mm to 12" 305mm. Everything was made to this scale so that, when standing together, they were all in order. Using this method, I made stage-coaches, complete with horses, passengers and luggage, and Noah's arks complete with figures, animals and birds.

I carved larger animals and dogs for special commission, one of which was the complete pack of beagles, for a master of hounds. I was still connected with scouting, and produced 'Kein' and all the animals from Kipling's *Jungle Book*.

Royalty

The Northern Counties Jamboree was held at Raby Castle, Co. Durham, in 1936. I carved a large stock of all my subjects for this show and they were a sell out. It was from connections I made there that I got a commission to carve a 'Corgi' dog for the present Queen Mother, then our Queen, and a Goosegirl, driving a flock of geese, for Princess Elizabeth, now our Queen.

Root carvings of snakes

Chaffinch. Cock pheasant. Hoopoe. Relief carvings. Painted yellow pine

From around that time, I did not carve again until about 1980. Then once more I started carving decoys. These have gone all over the world but mainly to America. In the autumn of 1989 I had a very successful show of Duck and Shorebird

Water cart with Clydesdale horse in painted yellow pine

decoys at the 'Rona' Gallery in New Bond Street.

That year I also did practical carving at an exhibition of Woodland Crafts held at 'Brantwood', the John Ruskin Museum in the Lake District.

Over the many years, I kept all my drawings of birds and animals packed away in a chest. Just after Christmas 1991, a gentleman called to see me. He said he had brought some old carvings to show me. From a tin box, he unpacked a huntsman on a grey horse, six fox hounds, and a running fox, and set them out on my table saying 'Now there's some carving for you'. I replied, 'You won't believe this but I carved those pieces myself about 50 years ago'. To this he replied 'No, you didn't, I bought these in the Lakes and you never lived there'. 'That's correct,' I said, 'but all our holidays were spent there — I did the carvings in the winter evenings and sold them to the gift shops in the summer.'

Only two days before I had got my drawings out of the chest. He was convinced when I showed him the original drawings. They fitted his carvings exactly. He then exchanged them with me for a painting of a Peregrine Falcon that I had done.

This episode has started me off carving the hunting figures again. I have had some of my yellow pine blocks sawn up into appropriate thicknesses. I trace the drawings onto the wood and fret saw them out, and glue, and do the carving with 'Stanley' slimline knives. Very little sanding is needed, as sharp cuts and edges give the effect of muscles, life and movement to the carvings. It is a great challenge to me at almost 78 years of age.

Carving keeps me young! ∎

Woodcock. Osprey with fish. Partridge. Relief carvings in yellow pine, finished with wax polish

WHAT COMES NATURALLY

Dayl Gable's carved vessels are inspired by the natural world, as David Ellsworth reports

Dayl Gable comes to woodcarving with a refreshing, natural ability. He studied portraiture and drawing in the 1960s, but has worked as a carpenter for the past twenty years. He loves Chinese jade carving, but has not been exposed to or influenced by the luminaries of contemporary woodcarving. As a result he remains free to translate his ideas, concepts and ideologies directly into his sculptures.

The vessel has become the foundation stage in Gable's work, from which everything else grows. His carvings show a keen understanding of the natural world and the many creatures that inhabit it. They are wonderfully graceful, playful, contented creatures, frozen in a frame of the mind's eye, doing what comes naturally. This interconnectedness, the 'vessel of nature' supporting life on land, sea and in the air, is the primary strength behind his imagery.

As Gable himself says: 'I try to translate my joy of the natural world into these pieces, and to be conscious of how even the tiniest detail can affect the whole.'

Party of River Otters, 13 x 6½in, 330 x 165mm, cherry burl. 'Like teenagers at a pool on a hot day, these otters like to have fun. Even though this piece took me about 60 hours to carve, I had a blast too.'

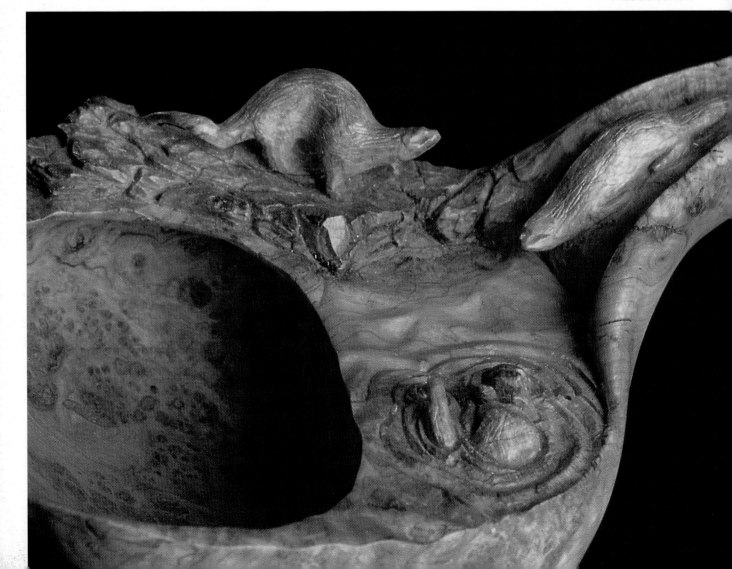

Visions of Native American Flutes,
1¼in diameter x 24in,
32mm diameter x 610mm,
white and red cedar and
various types of burl.

Dayl Gable writes: 'In 1991, after
crossing paths with American Indian
ways, I made twelve of these flutes.
The carved birds honour the
woodpecker who, according to

Plains Indian legend, gave the first
flute to a lovesick brave. I enjoyed
carving the birds so much that I
began exploring other avenues of
this craft.'

World Below His Wings,
8¼ x 8in, 210 x 200mm,
maple and African blackwood.
'The mountains and river below
this red-tailed hawk sustain
him. In return, like all predators,
he keeps the life below in
balance. Held in both hands,
the piece feels very
comfortable, especially when
contemplating this balance.'

Left *Feast from the Oaks*,
6in, 150mm diameter,
oak burl and African blackwood.
'On a bright autumn afternoon,
most of us have seen this little
creature, under an oak among
the dry leaves. He seems as
comfortable as you or I in a
soft chair enjoying a sandwich.'

Goose with an Attitude,
12 x 6in, 305 x 150mm,
cherry burl, guarea and
African blackwood.
'Looking back it's hard to
believe: this mere bird, this
goose, is going on the attack.
Panic! Cover up your
tender parts and run.'

Left **Forest Floor**,
9½ x 8½in, 240 x 215mm,
cherry, padauk and guarea.
'This vessel was excavated
from a partially overgrown
branch. In the forest during
summer drizzle, poke around,
and among the ferns, tucked
in a wet log, you might find this,
a glistening salamander.'

Dayl Gable

CLASSIC STYLE DECOYS

KEN BEYNON

Derek Richards carves ducks in the style of antique hunting decoys from the east coast of the USA.

Ken Beynon has been a committee member of the British Decoy and Wildfowl Carvers Association since its formation in 1990 and is the editor of its magazine. Like many others he became interested in decoy carvings when on a visit to the USA, and subsequently received tuition from the great Bob Ridges. He mainly carves decorative wildfowl and shorebirds, and received an award at the Pensthorpe Exhibition in the Autumn of 1993 for the best British waterfowl. Ken is fully retired after 35 years as a research chemist and manager with Shell.

1991 and again at Great Missenden in 1992.

Derek was born in London and although a city boy he developed a keen interest from an early age in art, natural history and bird-watching. He was an enthusiastic amateur photographer at school, and went on to the Regent Street Polytechnic School of Photography to study art and later photography. Derek has since become a successful advertising and travel photographer, with a

Dowitchers, heads joined to body with sliding dovetails. Highly commended in the 1991 BDWCA Championships

Derek Richards has been a member of the Committee of the British Decoy and Wildfowl Carvers Association (BDWCA) since its formation. He is also a regular winner in competitions for decoy carvers. He won two first prizes at Crewe in 1989. He won the Open Class for carved working decoys at Slimbridge in

studio and home in Kensington. All this was excellent grounding for another interest that he was about to discover.

In the early 80's, with his wife Rosemary, he spent two years living and working in California. On an assignment to Alaska they saw and heard, in the wild, a Great Northern Diver — a Loon as they still call it there. Derek later bought a Loon decoy as a

Derek Richards with one of his stylish birds

present for Rosemary, and it was this that established his interest in the making of decoys.

He read up the fascinating history of the early settlers in North America, and the part played in their lives by the working decoy. He was determined to find out more about the making and the makers of these beautiful wooden sculptures.

It might be said that these hunting decoys are America's original folk art. It has been claimed that they were devised by the native Indians to lure the ducks within range of their bows and arrows. Theirs were made out of a straw frame with bird skins stretched over the frame. The earliest known Indian decoys of this sort date from 1000 AD, and were found in a cave in Nevada in 1974. The early European settlers are believed to have copied this method of decoying, but used carved wooden birds instead. These proved to be a lot simpler than coping with the netted tunnel of the Dutch-type of decoy that they may have known; even if appropriate ponds could have been found to use in such a large landscape. The carved decoy proved to be the salvation of many an early colony. One occasion was in 1630, when in Plymouth, Massachusetts the settlers brought down a large and unexpected migratory flight of Snow Geese — enough

Pintail drake preening, 2nd prize winner in the senior class of the 1989 European Wildfowl Carving Championships

for a feast and to salt down to last them through the coming harsh winter.

On returning to the UK Derek met and studied with Bob Ridges. Through him he met Mark McNair who is arguably America's leading, contemporary carver of working-style decoys. This meeting proved to be a turning point. Like most UK bird carvers, Derek started as a 'detailer', but he didn't find the carving of decoratives as creative as he wished. Meeting Mark McNair, and working with him, introduced Derek to the traditional ways of carving, where character

and style are more important than anatomical accuracy.

Derek spends much time in the planning stage of each carving, including the photography of live birds and the preparation of sketches of the proposed carving. He seeks further inspiration in the excellent reference books that exist on the work of early American decoy carvers. He does not produce patterns, but prefers to transfer his sketches directly on to the wood.

He uses few power tools and carves mainly with axe, rasps and knives. Most of his work is now carved out of atlantic white cedar (*Chamaecyparis thyoides*), one of the traditional American decoy woods that he has had to import himself. It is straight-grained, easily worked with hand tools and does not rot. It is light in weight and has a glorious smell when worked. All his ducks are hollow, are weighted and float correctly.

From planks approximately 2" 50mm thick (in the case of ducks) the outline of the upper and lower halves of the body are cut out, using a band saw. The head is cut out separately. The two halves of the body are screwed together temporarily and are carved to near the desired shape. The usual tools Derek uses for this are an old but very sharp American 'roofers' hatchet, found in an antique shop in Vermont, and a draw knife. The halves are then separated and hollowed out. Having carved the head, using only a knife, it is attached to the body and the whole is pinned and glued ready for final carving with chisels, rasps and knives. There is the minimum of sanding. Rasp and join marks are deliberately left to show the nature of the wood.

Early decoys were painted very basically. When 'market gunning' was banned in 1918 the hunter-carvers found that they could make more money carving for a living than shooting, then they started to carve and paint more elaborate birds. With this history in mind Derek uses oil-based paints with a small range of colours — just black, white and brown. No sealing is done, so as to allow the paint to seep into the wood. When freshly painted the colours are naturally bright, and some closely-guarded tricks are used to 'age' (not antique) the carvings.

Derek has been carving in this style for some five years, and his success can be gauged from the number of his competition wins. He exhibits in various galleries and his work has also been on the BDWCA stands at many of the shows in recent years.■

BISON

DESIREE HAJNY

Desiree Hajny's interest in woodcarving began when she taught art for six years in a small Nebraska cattle-ranching community. Today she is regarded by many as America's finest animal carver.

Bison require no detailed description to anyone familiar with the history of the North American West. Bison were intimately connected with the settling of the western frontier. Bison are the largest terrestrial animal native to North America; they sometimes are called buffalo.

The carving

Trace the full-size pattern onto a 4½" 112mm high by 6" 150mm long and 3" 75mm wide piece of wood, with the grain running vertically. Cut out on the bandsaw.

Begin carving by removing excess wood until your rough has the curves and contours in the drawings and photograph.

The face of the bison is important. Draw the centre line from the top of the nose to between the ears, the drawing shows the centre line. The centre line goes down the centre of the skull to where the neck connects to it, (marked on the top view with a circle). After trimming the excess wood on the head from the top view and front view, draw a centre line from the top of the head to the end of the nose. Place

Bison side view

Bison plan view

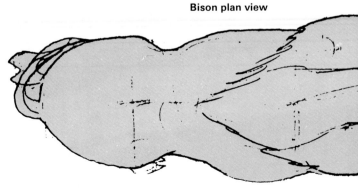

your pencil alongside of this line. It should measure approximately to the inside of the eye socket (this socket is where the eyeball, eye lid and muscles that operate the eye are located) and approximately the width of the muzzle.

Placing the pencil against the new line and splitting that distance in half will show you where the outside of the eye socket and the cheek bone is. It will also show the deep part of the ear, and the connection of the horn to the skull. From this line measure another pencil width, you'll find it hits the outside of the ear, if it's turned forward. It also shows, approximately, the distance the horns protrude from the head (each animal will vary).

The chart will guide you. The surface texture drawing will let you plan out the face. From the front view the head is five pencil widths wide and six pencil widths high (or long). Using the drawings follow the directions on each part of the face, eye, nose and ears.

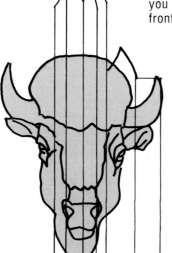

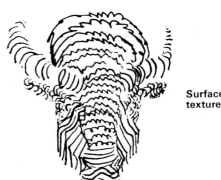

Surface texture

EARS AND EYES

Front   Side

Ears
1. Draw up shape of ear

2. Hollow out ear with veiner or rotary ball

3. Shape up back of ear

4. Woodburn edges using hairtract

1. Draw up and stop cut around eye shape.

2. Inverted pyramid by tear duct, then undercut the brow

3. Undercut eyeball under the lids rounding eyeball out

4. Sear eyeball with edges of burner point and burn following hairtract

NOSE

Side   Front

1. Draw up nose

2. V-cut nostrils and mouth

3. Undercut chin and shape up beard, then texture with a flat disk or V-cut

4. Woodburn (sear nose pad)

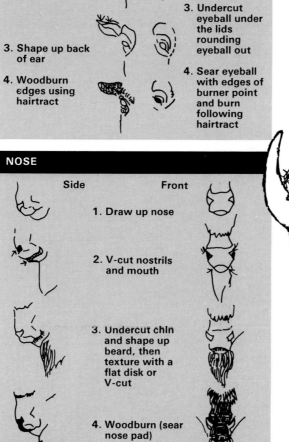

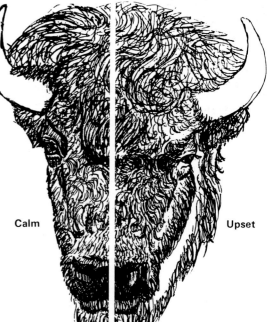

Calm   Upset

After the face is carved start concentrating on the front legs. They are 'hanging' from the body. Shape up this area referring to the pattern. The shoulders and scapula are tapered toward the spine, marked by the centre line. Use a gouge to sink this in.

The stomach area also tapers from the spine. It is rounded toward the bottom. Texture the lower area. Remember that gravity will pull the skin downward, so taper the heavy hair hanging there with a combination of gouges and veiners to give it a nice texture.

The pelvis area tapers just slightly from the spine. The hip will bulge out as marked on the pattern. The knee will stick out, then fold back into the lower leg (knee to heel). Using the chart, proceed with the shaping of the lower legs and feet.

The tail is textured, and at the end there is a tassle; somehow have it connected to the bison's body so it isn't a breakable area. Check over the Bison, and compare it to the pattern.

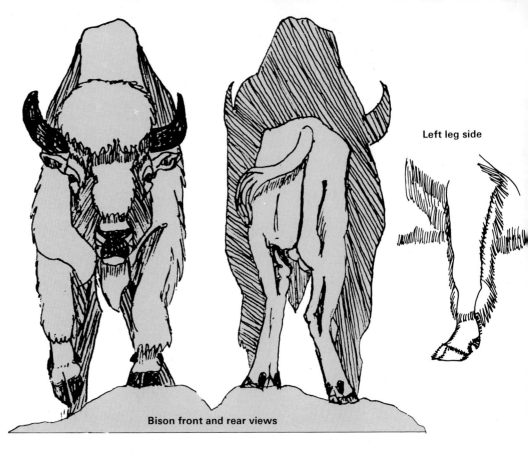
Bison front and rear views

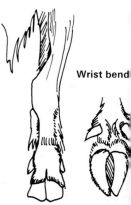

Left leg side

Wrist bend

Woodburning

Make small layers by using marks, referring to the hair tract as a guide. An adjustable woodburner, (one with a thermostat), is recommended for best results. Any tip that comes to a point will help with small hairs on the face, (with the exception of the writing tip).

Use a fluid 'stab-pull' motion and avoid putting in too many straight lines. Gravity pulls the fur, and the fur follows the contours of animal planes (use the chart for reference).

For heavily textured areas pull the burner tip deep across and along the deep areas of veiner or V-cuts. Then pull the burner tip from one deep area up over the high points and end up in another 'deep part' of the ravine (made by a V-cut or veiner).

To obtain shiny eyes sear the wood of the eyeball with the side of a hot burning tip. It will seal the wood as it darkens it. The final finish will sit on top of the seared areas and they will glisten. Sear the hooves and dew claws too.

A hint to help — mark in areas that are lighter with a pencil and draw in the direction of the fur. This serves as a guideline.

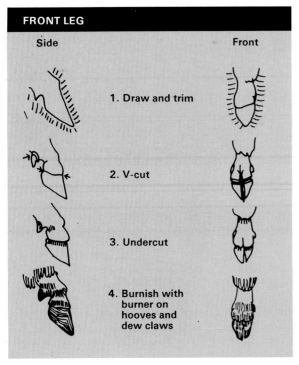

FRONT LEG

Side

Front

1. Draw and trim

2. V-cut

3. Undercut

4. Burnish with burner on hooves and dew claws

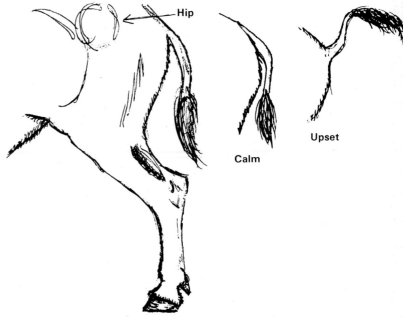

Hip

Calm

Upset

Bison hair tract

colours left on the pallette on the base. This way the colours will work with the animal. Mammals have colours that blend in with their habitat.

Drybrush areas on the animal to set off texture and to show where the sun is hitting the bison. Drybrushing is when the brush has just a hint of colour in the bristles — colour only high points. Drybrush on base also.

Use a detail round brush to paint the eyes and nose of the bison. Clean out the brush and put a tiny point of light paint on the top of the eye, here sun hits the eyeball. After the paint dries put a clear finish on.

The colouration of the bison is as follows: dark brown with long, shaggy, dark fur over the head, front shoulders and front legs, which is distinct from the short, smooth, light brown coat, with a tuft of big, black hairs on the tip of the tail. The head is massive and long hair extends over the throat to produce a beard. Both sexes have true horns, which are short, black, and gently curve upward. The calves are reddish when first born. Keep in mind that each one varies a bit. ∎

Painting

Whatever type of paint you choose keep it thinned so that the pigment doesn't clog up the texture worked in by the burner.

It is desirable to have the wood colour show through. Let the colours bleed together, (get pictures of a bison that show what colours you will need. Start with light colours and gradually work into the darker ones until you've hit black. Let these colours dry completely. Use up the

The first real memory Lee Dickenson has of carving comes from Woodwork Class at School. Given his chance, he did not look back and, although other jobs followed after school, he always knew what he wanted to do.

He has now been a self-employed carver for seven years, and has to date completed a wide range of carving and sculptural commissions, architectural work, new pieces and restoration; making new carved furniture and fittings as well as restoring and repairing existing items.

His greatest joy is to follow his own ideas with all manner of carvings. He now has work in private collections all over the United Kingdom as well as Europe, North America and as far afield as India.

Recognition of his skill has brought him a full workload, however, like most self-employed people he is always looking for the next opportunity. He has won numerous awards including Bronze, Silver and Gold Medals at National Woodworker Competitions.

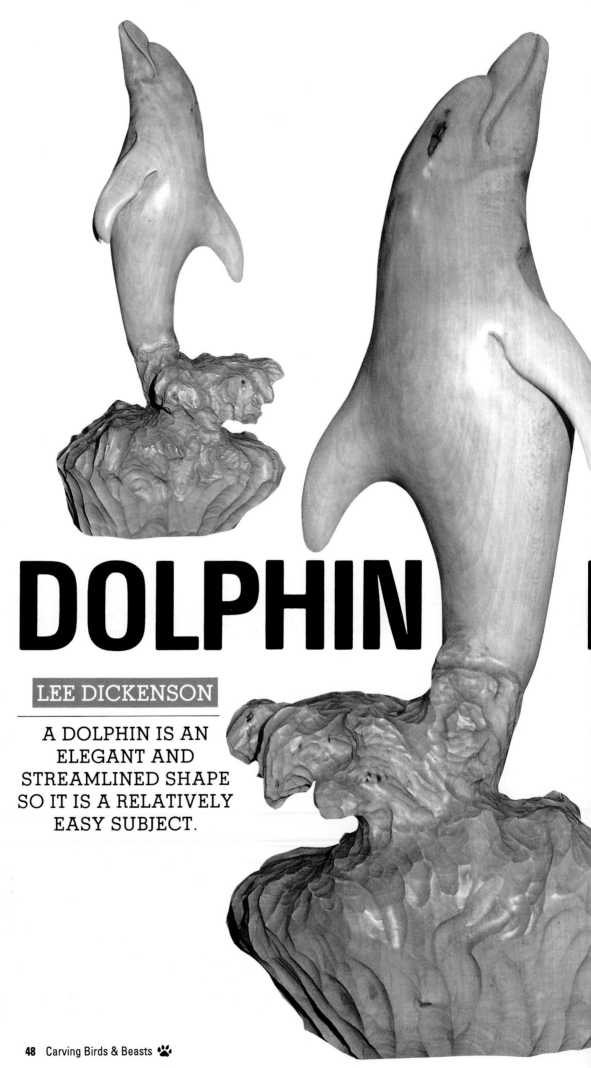

DOLPHIN

LEE DICKENSON

A DOLPHIN IS AN ELEGANT AND STREAMLINED SHAPE SO IT IS A RELATIVELY EASY SUBJECT.

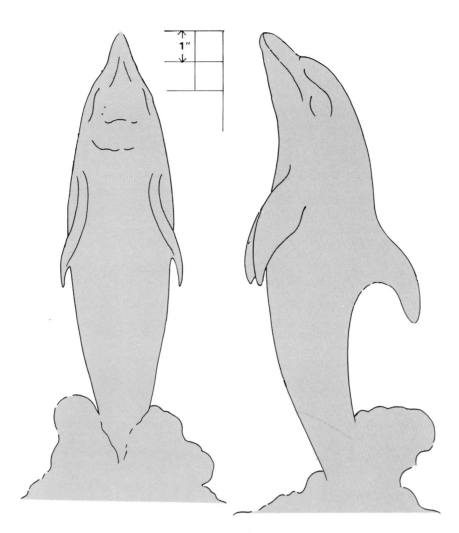

1"

N THE WAVES

I have tried to show the dolphin in a pose familiar to us all. High out of the water on its tail, moving backwards in a way that is supposed to be an expression of playfulness.

This is a simple carving because of the dophin's lack of fiddly details. It will be noticed that I did not carve in the eyes, mainly because dolphins' eyes are very small. Another reason is that the timber I had was marked naturally on one side of the dolphin's head, and I felt that this confused the scene. If you want to add detail, the water can become as complicated as you wish.

Timber

The timber used was lime wood. I chose this for its ease of carving, little grain effect and smoothness of finish. This is not to say that a highly figured timber, with distinctive streaks, would not be suitable; streaks could help convey the movement and form of the animal.

Drawing and marking out

After preparing drawings of side and front views, they were applied using carbon paper, to the chosen squared block, then it was ready to be bandsawn out. I always find it easier if the smoother of the drawn lines is cut first, as the waste can be more accurately replaced to reclaim the drawing for the next cut. In this case the front of the dolphin had the smoothest line, so I cut

this, then taped it back in place.

I had too large a blade at the time and had to leave a lot of waste around the dorsal fin.

A high-ground guidance line running down the body on all sides is helpful to mark the high areas. Drawing on of the details like the front fins, using a ruler or dividers to mark-off from the drawing, is essential. Having spent time getting it right on the drawings it makes sense to make full use of them.

Holding and carving

The work needs to be held firmly while carving; a vice is useful, but a hydra-clamp or a similar workholder makes for ease of work, but it's not essential.

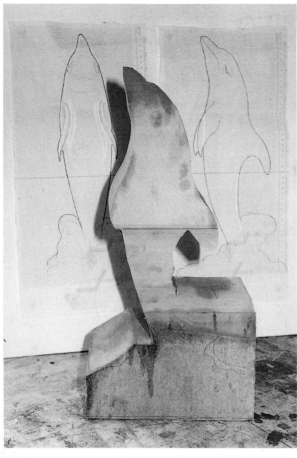

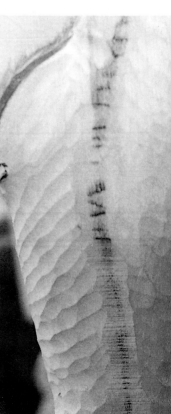

The drawings were traced on to the wood and a bandsaw removed the bulk of the waste; the blade was too wide to get behind the fin

The corners are rounded towards the high-ground line and the waste between the front fins has been extracted

If a vice is the only workholder being used some thought must be be given to later work around the base; you cannot clamp what you want to work on. Either extra length must be included in the base block and sawn-off later, or other material can be screwed to the underside of the base and this is held in a vice or clamped to the bench.

The body of the dolphin could be clamped, but it would make for difficulties in access, and careful packing would be needed to prevent any wood bruising; careful placement of clamps would be required as well to prevent fins from being broken!

As mentioned earlier the shape is simple and streamlined, the carver having only to round the body off. My usual beginning is to incise a line to the outside of a detail line, using a V-tool. This allows the waste to be chopped

A high-ground line marks the top of the curve of the dolphin's round body, hatching marks the waste to be removed

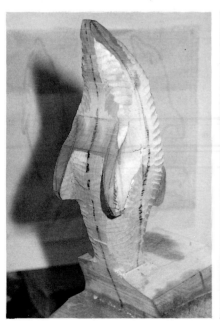

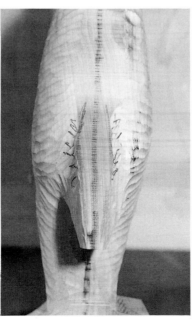

The dorsal fin is refined

Waste marked ready for the coping saw to cut a more curved shape

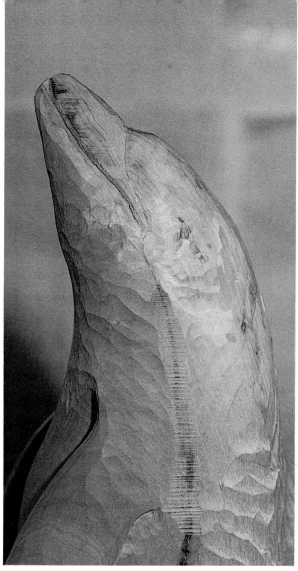

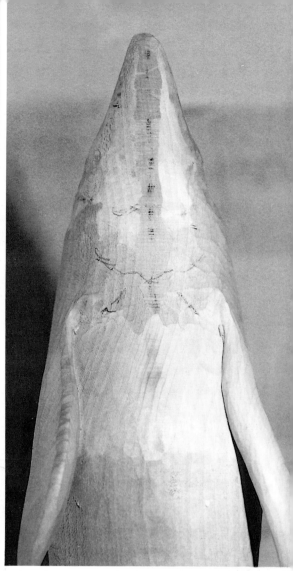

The detail of the head drawn on ready for carving

The top of the head formed into a smooth curve

Modelling in the rolls of fat on the dolphin's 'neck'; the fins are nearly finished now

out with little risk of tearing material away from a portion that should be left, for example the front fins.

The main operation in this piece is rounding the body, not flattening. Working initially from the corners, gradually work towards the high-ground line. The rounded shape will begin to emerge, but should not be finished-off at this point.

The dorsal fin can be shaped but again not finished. Leave a little material now, so the whole body can be moulded and brought together in proportion in the later stages. The waste left from my lazy bandsawing was cleaned out at this point; I used a coping saw though it could have been carved out.

The areas around the front fins can now receive more attention, to relieve them and begin preliminary shaping. A flat chisel was used to pare down the sharp line inside the fin. Gouging evened up the thickness of the fin. Then similar treatment was given to the other fin. I finished off with some paring to just slightly round

over the fins and tuck them in at the body joint.

The details of the head can be drawn in including the mouth, eye areas and the characteristic forehead bulge. The lines are again cut in with a V-tool; the smaller the better. With a small gouge model around the lower jaw, round off the upper jaw and forehead, and relieve the eye mounds. The study of drawings and research photographs is helpful to mould the head into the typical dolphin shape.

The final shape of the body can now be considered. In common with a great many creatures — myself included — the dolphin's body is slightly flatter and fatter along the underside, and certainly there are one or two rolls of fat that need to be modelled in. The whole body should be pared down with a flat chisel, or flattish gouge, to clean up the deeper gouge cuts.

The base waves

The base area represents a flurry of water, created by the dolphin as it vigorously ploughs backwards. In my carving it's the hardest part, but also fun. There are, of course, as many different interpretations of water as there are drops of water in the sea. The style I chose, I feel, is not entirely successful. You may feel you need a whole ocean of the stuff, or just the merest suggestion. The flow of the grain could have been employed to suggest upward movement.

I set about marking my interpretation and clearing a V-area to the front of the dolphins; a V-tool and a skew chisel formed this area. The block was rounded off, and swirling, fairly large random grooves were cut out.

The sides were chopped down, the tools manipulated to create the effect of the water (to prevent damage to the gouge, chopping down was not done on the hydra-clamp). A narrower gouge, with

The body of the dolphin smoothed by flat chisels and shallow gouges

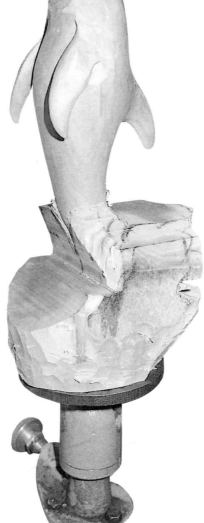

The base rounded off and the waves beginning to take shape

The flutes on the base were cut with a deep fluted gouge chopping down; this was done off the metal base of the workholder

high sides to prevent digging-in, was then randomly chased around the first series of gouge cuts, to form a secondary set of grooves. A forward bent spoon gouge, used in a short scooping action, broke up the previous grooves to give the effect. Where the water parts around the front of the dolphin it has a much lighter treatment.

Finishing

Once satisfied with the base, the whole carving can be cleaned up by fine paring and/or sanding. Thin curved riffler files helped to clean around the fins, though a piece of folded sandpaper would do just as well.

I finished my dolphin with a couple of coats of button polish, for some reason best known to the creator! It gave a 'nice' finish, but I personally am not too sure whether it suits the subject. A more transparent finish or even bleaching might have been a better choice. ∎

The surface smoothed with abrasive paper; riffler files were used under the fins

MARE AND FOAL

REG PARSONS SHOWS HOW TO CARVE A SCENE OF EQUINE AFFECTION

Horses have captured the imagination of artists and carvers through the ages. Early cave paintings and carvings often depicted horses. They have been admired and even worshipped for their exciting vitality. This carving is an attempt to show the beauty of a mare, the endearing quality of a foal and the bond of affection between them.

The mare is standing with her back to the wind, her tail and mane blowing forward. She is turning her head to keep an eye on the foal nestled between her legs. It is, I think, a balanced pose – economic with wood and structurally strong. For the sake of clarity, the side view drawing doesn't show that the left fore-leg of the mare is attached to the foal, but it is clear in the photographs.

The foal adds support to one of the vulnerable legs and reinforces the fact that the whole piece is carved from one block of wood. If you have sufficient wood it would be better if the grain was running vertically, up the legs, but like many others I have to make do with what I have in store.

The wood

The wood used was ash (*Fraxinus excelsior*), which is hard and difficult to carve, even with the sharpest tools. The grain was unusually wild and obtrusive, detracting from the detail of the carving. Altogether it was a bad choice for this carving – I have used ash many times before with better results. Superior pale wood for this perhaps would be sycamore (*Acer pseudoplatanus*) or one of the other maples (*Acer species*), or lime (*Tilia vulgaris*). Darker woods such as walnut (*Juglans regia*) and elm (*Ulmus procera*) could also be used, though elm is often wild grained and detail might be lost.

You will see that the base in the drawing is more abstracted than the one in the photographs. I have done this to stress that you shouldn't copy the base, or the

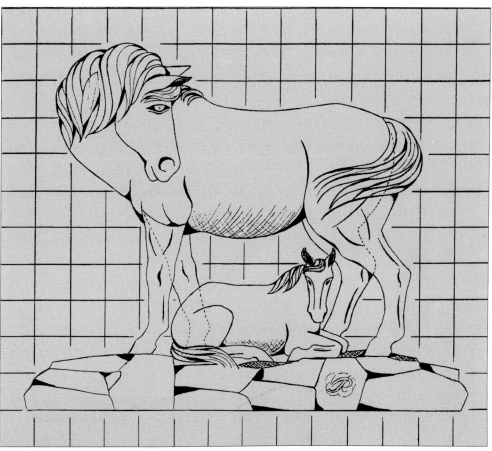

vice, but eventually it will need to be worked on and you will have nothing to hold. A block screwed under the base is a simple solution, but I recommend a 'tall' T-shaped block. The top of the T-shape should be about 2½in, 63mm square, and the stem about 5in, 125mm long and 1½in, 38mm square. Screws through the lip at the top of the T-shape go into the work, and the long stem allows the carving to be tilted as well as rotated in the vice.

If available, remove the waste outside the drawn outline with a bandsaw. Otherwise you can do this with a handsaw, cut across the grain at about ¾in, 20mm intervals close to the line, then split the wood away between the cuts with a gouge and mallet — say a ⅝in, 15mm No.7. The ragged surface can be cleaned up with a round Surform.

You will have to redraw the outline as you cut it away, and you should also draw in the line of the spine on top of the neck and back, and the centre line of the face. I

Mare and foal side projection

Left **Blocked out ready for bosting in**

Right **Centrelines on the head, back and legs help to keep the proportions right**

rest of the carving exactly. The result would be dull and uninteresting, as you would be paying too much attention to the drawings and not enough to the wood. If you intend to carve a base similar to the one in the photographs, leave enough wood round the rear hooves, as they are buried in the grass. Gouge sweeps mentioned are the ones I used, but similar sweeps and sizes would be as useful.

Wood preparation

Before I start carving I clean up the surface of the wood, so that I can see any knots or shakes that will have to be avoided. This also reveals any grain figure that can be incorporated in the design. You can then transfer the drawing on to the prepared block.

At this stage the holding method should be considered. Initially the base could be held in a

also find it useful to draw in the centre lines of the legs.

When the outline has been established the wood under the mare's belly can be removed, either by drilling then carving, or with a jigsaw. Don't try to separate the two fore legs, or the rear legs, until later. Block in the foal, ensuring that it remains firmly attached to the mare's left foreleg. Don't round over any of the carving until the outline is established.

Bosting in

During the bosting in (establishing the shape from the rough outline), heavy blows on the top of the work could well damage the legs. In these circumstances a stout canvas bag about 15x15in,

380x380mm, partially filled with a mixture of dry builders' sand and sawdust, can be used to support the carving. The work will bed into the bag, which will cushion the vulnerable areas from the shock of heavy mallet blows.

When you are actually shaping the carving, photographs and pictures of foals and mares should be studied and referred to during the whole carving process. Only by careful study do you stand a chance of making a lively and realistic carving. Remember to leave extra wood where the tail is blown across the rump and on the right-hand side of the neck for the mane. Both the mane and forelock are slightly exaggerated for a more wind blown effect.

With the body shapes established, the shape of the legs can be

properly judged and adjusted if necessary. Once the outline of the legs is correct, the wood between them can be removed. I drilled the bulk of the waste out first, then used a ⅜in, 10mm No.10 gouge. Great care needed to be taken here, as the gouge was cutting along the grain and the wood could easily split away.

Shaping the foal's back is difficult because of its position under the mare. I found that a front bent ⅜in, 10mm gouge was the best tool for this.

The base

As you carve down the legs of the mare, and round the foal, you will need to define where they meet the base. This is a good time to carve the rest of the base. The base

Working down the mare to the foal, note the extra material allowed for the tail

illustrated in the photographs is the product of my imagination. The base in the drawing should be first roughed out with a ⅝in, 15mm No.7 gouge. Make it as irregular as possible, narrowing it at the ends and between the mare's legs. The rock could be defined with a ¼in, 6mm No.9 gouge, then facets could be cut at all angles with a ⅜in, 10mm No.3. You may have to repeat this several times to get a dramatic effect.

The head

On my carving only the mare's left eye is visible, the other is covered by her forelock. However, it occurred to me after bosting in that the forelock could, quite reasonably, have flowed over the other eye instead. Thus putting the visible eye where it would be easier to carve, without detracting from the overall effect.

The base is shaped round the mare's feet and the foal

Ready for polishing

To create the eyeball I used a length of ¼in, 6mm steel rod with a spherical hollow drilled in the end. This was pushed straight into the wood, then a small triangle was cut in at the front and rear of the eyeball using a ⅛in, 3mm No.3 gouge – a sharp craft knife would do. The eye was brought to life with a small hole drilled in the eyeball to represent the pupil.

The mouth was carved with a ⅟₁₆in 1.5mm No.10 veiner. Wood below and above the mouth was reduced with a ¼in 6mm No.6 gouge to form the lips. Once the mouth has been carved the space left for the nostrils should be obvious. They should be defined with a ⅛in, 3mm No.10 veiner, taking great care not to crumble the edges by making a series of shallow cuts. Make the nostrils stand proud of the nose by removing wood from around the outside edge with a ⅜in, 10mm No.6 gouge.

blades can also be ground into scrapers. Small scrapers are invaluable for cleaning up small difficult areas like this, and can even be used for small amounts of final shaping.

Use scrapers to remove gouge marks then sand with reducing grades of abrasives, finishing with 600 grit wet and dry paper used dry. Be careful not to round over crisply carved areas in the tail and mane.

Remove all traces of dust and burnish the wood with a lint free cloth, then give the whole carving a coat of sanding sealer, including under the base. The sanding sealer will show up any areas of roughness in difficult to reach areas, such as in the ears and round the eyes. You may need to tackle these with scrapers and abrasives again. Obviously, any areas you work on will need to be re-coated with sealer.

When the sanding sealer is dry it will need to be denibbed – specks of dust that settled on the surface as it dried will have to be removed. This is best done lightly with some well worn fine abrasive paper, so you don't sand through the finish. Finish off with several layers of wax polish to build up a soft lustre. ∎

The mane

To represent the mane being blown by the wind, it is thicker on the right-hand side. Mark on the main hanks of hair and define them deeply with a ⅜in, 10mm No.10 fluter. Round over the edges with a ⅜in, 10mm No.3 gouge. This will have to be repeated a number of times to get down to the required depth. With the main hanks defined, draw on lines flowing across the surface, then carve them in with a ¼in, 6mm No.9 gouge. In the spaces between these cuts make a few random lines following the flow of the hair, with a small quick gouge, say a ⅛in, 3mm No.10.

The tail is carved similarly to the mane, except that the main channels all flow from the root of the tail to the tip. Remember to make sure that the foal's tail and mane flow in the same direction.

Draw on the muscles and bones, as shown on the drawing and outline them with a ¼in, 6mm No.9 gouge. Use a ¼in, 6mm No.3 gouge to remove the waste wood round the muscles, then contour them smoothly into the legs and body with a small scraper.

The mane is deeply carved in a flowing pattern

The windswept mane is the main feature in this view

Small scrapers have to be home made, as far as I know they are not commercially available. Cut a tapering strip from a cabinet scraper – ½in, 13mm tapering to ¼in, 6mm – then grind the ends to suitable curves. Broken hacksaw

To carve an animal is one thing, but to carve a likeness of a particular animal is quite another. George Brownlee used to paint portraits, so he has learnt to observe the small differences in features which make a person into that particular person.

With dogs, George looks for variations in the shape of the eyes, the hooding of eyelids, length of the nose and type of fur. He describes how long-haired dogs 'wear' their fur, whereas short fur is close to the skull. A portrait must be built up, he says: 'You simply can't do caricatures of people's pets.'

distract the dog with a sweet and take a top view. Armed with these profile shots and using a broomhandle as a support, you make a model in plasticine. To carve at all you must have some idea of perspective, and at least with this material you can put back what you have taken off.

George's dog heads have all been made into walking sticks, so the size of the head is determined by what is comfortable to hold. He then works on the proportions, using the photographs.

Next stage is to transfer the measurements to a paper pattern. Carving instruction books do not generally help

here. Some carvers make a pattern by taking different views from the same distance, then draw a grid over the photos and draw out the shape. This can be a problem with dogs as they do move about a lot. So George works from the completed model.

Making a pattern

To do this you need graph paper with ½in squares, sliding callipers, a ruler and a set square. The set square is laid flat next to the model so that the ruler and the callipers can be laid against it to keep the measurements accurate.

Paper pattern for a labrador. Once the plasticine model is complete, accurate measurements are taken and marked on a ½in grid to build up the picture

George Brownlee carves dogs that are as individual as people. Here he talks to Judith Nicoll

PET I

Look and learn

Success is not just based on artistic talent but also on skills that can be acquired. First of these is observation. How wide is the muzzle? How long the snout? At what level of the snout bone are the eyes set? Eyes are set at different angles and eyelids at different levels. Each detail relates to the other to build up a three-dimensional portrait. It is not just the habitually mournful expression of your labrador watching you eat your dinner that distinguishes him from other dogs.

George does feature noticeable habits, such as the dog that always has one ear up and the other down, or another that always has its tongue out. But having carved several dogs of the same breed, he knows that they vary as much as people: 'jowls droop, ears vary and hang as differently as finger-prints'.

Modelling

The first task is to take many photographs. You need some for character and some of the four profiles: left, right, from the front and back. It is also helpful to

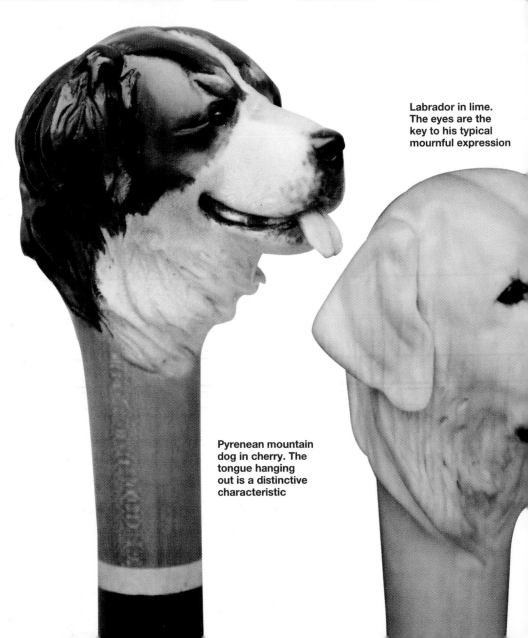

Labrador in lime. The eyes are the key to his typical mournful expression

Pyrenean mountain dog in cherry. The tongue hanging out is a distinctive characteristic

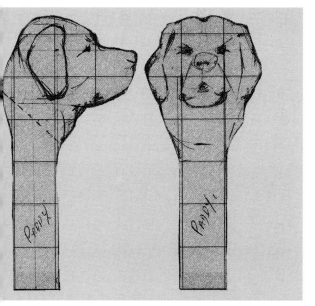

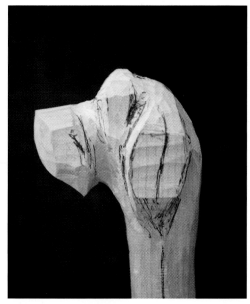

On this long-haired dachsund, the positions of the features are marked on the wood, using the paper pattern as a guide

ORTRAITS

George starts by taking the distance from the base to the top of the head on the side profile, and the centre of the head. Each measurement is then marked onto the paper. Once you have the centre of the head on both profiles you can measure away from it.

He then chooses different reference points, say an ear or the eye. He measures the length of the nose, the width between the eyes or the level of the eyes in relation to the snout bone.

Gradually the grid references build up like a map. This method can be applied to any figure and is one of the chief advantages of using a maquette.

Mirror of the soul

The eye is not only one of the key reference points but also an important element of character. As George reminds me, it is the mirror of the soul. When carving the eyes he first looks at the shape of the skull, and how the eyes sit in it, to determine their exact position. He measures from the tip of the nose to the centre of the eye, and marks the spot on to the side view. From

Father boxer in Canadian cherry, with dark areas stained

Daughter boxer – the same breed but a completely different dog. Lime with stain and bleach

the front or top he finds the width between the eyes. People are inclined to carve eyes flat, but heads are rounded and each eye goes round the corner a bit. The round eyeball does not lie inside a flat plane.

Dogs' eyes generally fit below the snout line and are set back in the skull. The hardest part is finding where eyes are socketed: keep referring back to your photographs and model. On dogs the eyeball is big, but be careful because people usually carve them too big anyway. George cites bears, which have tiny eyes in relation to their body mass.

When cutting out the eyeball, remember that the top and bottom curvatures must match, particularly when half closed. George chooses a gouge with the right sweep and size to cut straight into the head. He then uses it at a 45° angle to create a dome. He suggests practising the technique on the base.

Eyelids also give character – open or half-closed they can portray the mood. George suggests thinking of a sphere with the eyelids covering it. The pupil or iris position is vital to give the right expression, as he demonstrates with cartoon drawings of eyes looking up and down. But he admits

that on this size carving he does not bother to carve an iris.

Finishing touches

At the finishing stage, George uses a high-gloss waxy varnish on the eyes to create a wet look. On some dogs this can also be used inside the nostril or diluted on the tip of the nose.

He has built up an expertise with stains and bleach to create different effects on different woods, experimenting with colours, strengths and numbers of coats to achieve realistic fur patterns. He suggests practising on off-cuts first.

For example, he uses a dark stain on long-haired dogs and then wipes off the high spots with spirit. For the whisker holes on the muzzle he makes small holes with a needle, then stains with a pointed brush and quickly rubs off any extra to leave a little spot of dark in the hole. Again, observation is essential: there is a pattern to whiskers – they spiral out in lines towards the nostril.

He uses boiled linseed oil or sanding sealer, as appropriate to the wood. Bleached wood, such as on the dalmatians, is best sealed before stain is applied to adjacent areas.

Fitting ends

These heads are all set on walking sticks, which George started making after a visit to Pitlochry. The idea for pets' heads came from a suggestion for a family present for someone with boxer dogs. All subsequent dogs' heads came from this pair. There was an immediate demand.

In spite of the advice in this article to obtain photographs, George admits that his next commission was for a boxer already dead. The only picture was taken from 15ft away. Yet the client cried with recognition and pleasure when she saw it in George's workshop. Similarly the portrait of a long-haired dachshund living in Germany had to be produced from a single photograph.

The sticks are either turned or of natural cut, but George likes to put on dividing rings of a contrasting colour, usually in ebony or box, to set off the heads. These are carved on the short grain for good cleaning up. The carving is then screwed on to the stick. ∎

Dalmatian. Lime with stain and bleach

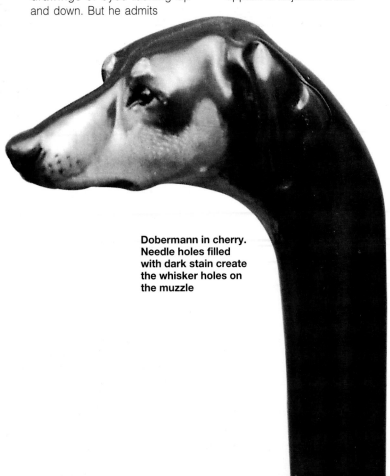

Dobermann in cherry. Needle holes filled with dark stain create the whisker holes on the muzzle

George Brownlee, aged 54, lives in Rochford in Essex and has been carving in his converted garage for ten years. He is interested in all forms of art and started sketching and painting at an early age. At ten he was painting portraits as a hobby, and later was commissioned to paint the heads of kings and queens for pub signs. He collected oriental carvings, and their intricacy inspired him to have a go. Self-taught, George now teaches carving to individuals or small groups in his workshop.

HUMPBACK HARMONY

ANDREW THOMAS' BREACHING HUMPBACK WHALE IS A PERSONAL STATEMENT ABOUT THE SEA

Andrew Thomas was born in 1963 and spent his early years in Australia, moving back to Dorset in 1969. After leaving school, he joined the Merchant Navy and travelled around the world. Wanting a change in life, he left the Navy.

When he met his wife-to-be, Andrew did not know how much she would change his life, because Christine is part Romany, and her culture held the start of Andrew's woodworking career.

With a small inheritance left to him, Andrew bought a traditional horse-drawn bow top caravan, which needed extensive restoration. Unable to find a capable craftsman, Andrew decided to attempt restoration himself. Before long, he was designing, making and restoring many types of horse-drawn vehicles, decorating them in the traditional style.

Five years and a biting recession later, Andrew decided to steer his career towards developing his woodcarving skill, as this aspect of his work was the most pleasurable and fulfilling. After attending a course given by Ian Norbury, Andrew is now devoted to his chosen craft.

Dimensions including stand: 23 x 20½ x 17in, 585 x 523 x 430mm the actual length of the whale from nose to tail is 25in, 635mm

My love of the sea and its inhabitants goes back to my early teens, when I was a keen sub-aqua diver. The original concept of carving a breaching humpback whale was exciting and important to me. Over the years, I have seen these intelligent, graceful creatures hunted to near extinction, and their environment polluted almost beyond repair.

First step was to gather as much information on humpback whales as possible, mainly from the local library, plus an excellent film I had acquired. Only two-dimensional information but very useful. Scale drawings were done next, based on this information, which told me the sizes of woods I needed.

The wood

My main supplier of wood is Yandle & Sons of Martock, who stock good quality wood at a fair price and are most helpful. There I selected a plank of American black walnut (*Juglans nigra*) 60 x 7 x 3in, 1525 x 180 x 75mm, for the whale; the piece for the tail flukes was 14 x 12 x 2½in, 355 x 305 x 63mm; the sea was lime, 22 x 18 x 3in, 560 x 460 x 75mm, all kiln dried.

Two pieces 22in, 560mm long were cut from the plank for the main part of the whale's body. For the middle section of the tail, one piece, 6 x 4 x 2½in, 150 x 100 x 63mm was cut from the 12in, 305mm board and the piece for the tail flukes was 12 x 8 x 2½in, 305 x 200 x 63mm.

Laminating was next, so the wood was planed top, bottom and sides, flat and square. This was done to minimise the glue line, aid good bonding and, very importantly, for accurate band-sawing. Using PVA, I first glued the two main parts of the body. The tail pieces, one at a time, were built up on the body, clamping all edges and surfaces as tightly as possible, and wiping away excess glue with a damp cloth.

Using my drawings and carbon paper, I drew the outline of the top view of the whale on to the top of the wood, then drew the outline of the side view on one side. This gave the necessary outline for bandsawing.

Bandsawing

The first cuts on the bandsaw were along the sides of the whale from the top view. I cut just outside the line and then taped the waste back on with masking tape to keep the block square. From the side view, the top and bottom outlines were then cut. On the underside of the whale, I left a small flat area that wasn't band-sawn, on to which I could glue a small piece of wood to screw into for mounting the whale on the

faceplate and vice.

Once mounted, I drew the centre line on top of the whale and marked on the sides the positions where the fins were to be dowelled. This gave me two measuring reference points. From here, using dividers and a vernier gauge, I marked off the centre, nearest, furthest, highest and lowest points of the eye and surround.

Carving

The blowholes are the highest point of the body, apart from the tail. Using my drawings, a $^3/_{16}$in, 5mm No. 3 gouge and a v-tool, I carved the blowholes to the correct depth and shape. Then, using a rotary burr, I made two clean, deep holes, tidying up with a diamond sphere burr. These completed, I was able to carve the correct angle down the nose, back and sides from the blowholes.

The widest point of the body is where I marked the centre points for the fins to be dowelled in. Then starting on the top edge of either side, using a ¾in, 19mm No. 5 gouge, I rounded the edges off the body and head, down to near the correct depth, leaving a little to carve in the detail. I then repeated this process on the underside, taking care, checking measurements and using reference points.

The centre of gravity is immediately in front of the whale's splash, giving an even distribution of weight, and stability

An average, fully grown humpback whale can have forty or more slits on its back

Fins

Blanks for the fins were cut from the plank to 7½ x 3½ x 3in, 190 x 90 x 75mm. I used my lathe to turn a 1¼ x ¾in, 32 x 19mm off-centre

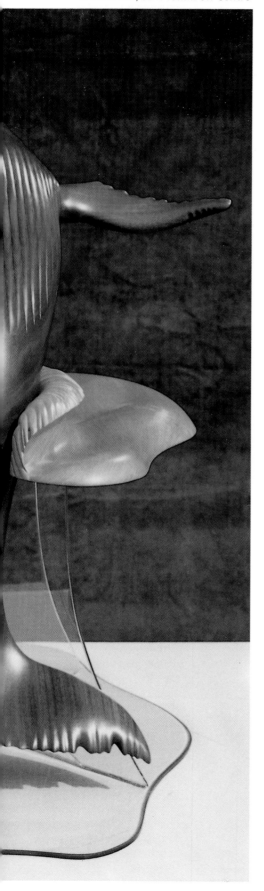

dowel at one end of each fin, then, using carbon paper, drew on the top and side view of the fins and cut out the waste. I decided that it would be better to carve the fins mounted on a separate piece of wood using the dowel as a temporary fixing. This way the joint would not get worn on the whale and every point was easier to reach.

When the fins were completed, I drilled a ¾in, 19mm hole on both sides of the body for the fins, and plugged them in without glue, then I drew around the edge of the fins where they meet the body. After removing the fins, I cut very carefully on the line, using gouges that matched its curvature. Working from the dowel hole outwards, I cut away the waste

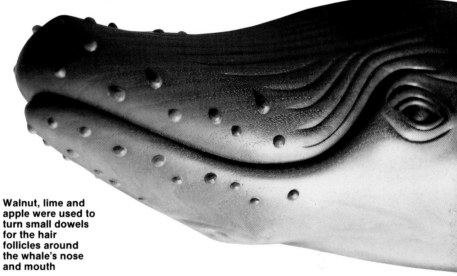

Walnut, lime and apple were used to turn small dowels for the hair follicles around the whale's nose and mouth

until I created a socket about ¼in, 6mm deep that matched the shape of the fin ends. The fins were then plugged in again to check, the ends disappearing into the body, giving a natural effect. I then removed the fins again; gluing them in position would be one of the last jobs as they would be very obstructive.

I started cutting in the details around the fin sockets on the body first, using a chip carving knife to cut the slits and a ³/₁₆in, 5mm No. 3 chisel to shape the wood into the slits. This led me to the eyes, all measurements, widths and depths checked, again using the knife to cut and chisels to shape. The main advantage of using the knife is that it cuts a deep slit, unlike the v-tool, so a disappearing cut can be created, rather than a groove, which in this area would be no good.

Mouth

Once happy with the eyes, I moved on to the mouth, again using the top centre line and the middle of the eye for measuring reference points. I marked accurately and drew in the mouth line, cutting with the knife and shaping with a ¼in, 6.5mm No. 6 and a ³/₁₆in, 5mm No. 3 gouge. I then finished off the chin and under the mouth area but without yet cutting in the belly slits.

The next stage was to prepare for inserting the hair follicles around the mouth and chin, so the whole area was sanded, using 80, 120, 150, 240 and 500 grit abrasives. I marked the points where I wanted the follicles, and using ⁵/₃₂, ³/₁₆ and ⁷/₃₂in, 4, 5 and 6mm woodbits, drilled holes ¼in, 6.5mm deep at these points. The woods I used for the follicles were walnut, lime and apple, turned on the lathe into small dowels a few inches long.

I wanted to keep the gluing tidy and an idea that worked well was to use a child's medicine syringe (without needle) bought at the chemist for 50p. This was filled with glue, the nozzle inserted into each hole and the syringe gently pressed. If too much glue came out, it was very easily sucked back into the nozzle, leaving no messy overspills. Using a mallet, the dowels were then gently tapped into the holes, cut off at the correct size and roughly shaped with a ³/₁₆in, 5mm No. 3 gouge.

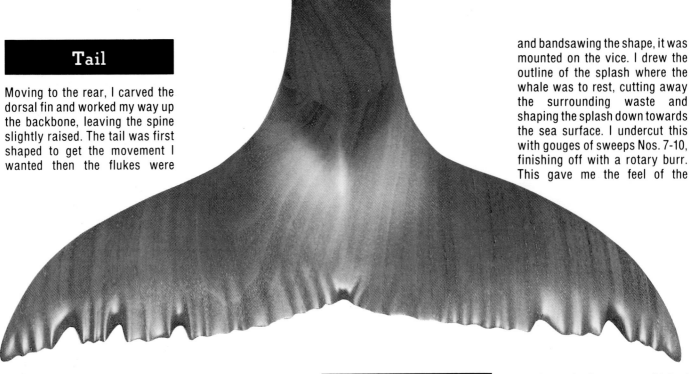

Tail

Moving to the rear, I carved the dorsal fin and worked my way up the backbone, leaving the spine slightly raised. The tail was first shaped to get the movement I wanted then the flukes were carved in, with gouges ranging from No. 3 to No. 7 sweep. The female genital area was cut with a knife and shaped with a $^3/_{16}$in, 5mm No. 3 gouge. On the underbelly nothing more could be carved until the block that I used to screw into was cut off. Before doing so, I sanded all reachable areas, with all grits, then, after taking the whale off the vice, I cut off the holding block.

Now I had access to the underbelly. This was shaped first, then the belly slits were drawn and cut with the knife and shaped with the $^3/_{16}$in, 5mm No. 3 gouge. I used spherical rotary burrs to produce and clean up the whale's navel. After sanding the area with all five grits, the whale was then ready for finishing.

Finishing

First I brushed on many applications of boiled linseed oil, which enhances the beautiful colour of black walnut. After the wood had soaked in as much as possible for a couple of days, I applied wax on top, giving many coats over a week or so. The end result was very pleasing, being smooth and glossy. When I was happy with the finish I glued the side fins into place and the whale was complete.

Top view over whale's splash, showing the inside shape and angle where the tail and dorsal fin slot in

Detail of flukes. Every whale has its own pattern of flukes on its tail, as individual as our own fingerprints

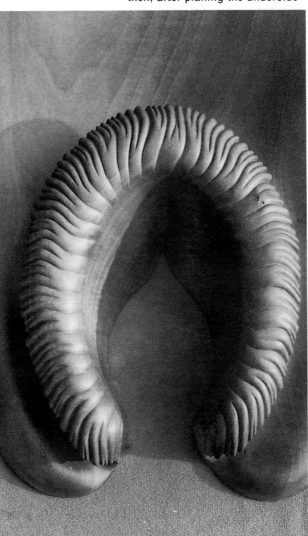

The sea

For the sea, using my drawings and carbon paper, I drew the outline of the sea on to my wood, then, after planing the underside and bandsawing the shape, it was mounted on the vice. I drew the outline of the splash where the whale was to rest, cutting away the surrounding waste and shaping the splash down towards the sea surface. I undercut this with gouges of sweeps Nos. 7-10, finishing off with a rotary burr. This gave me the feel of the motion of the sea, which I followed to produce gentle swells over the board.

To set the whale into the board of the sea, I had to hold it at the desired angle and take the profile of the upper and lower parts of the body that were to be inside the splash. This, carved accurately, would hold the whale in the sea without any securing or support.

I drew the upper and lower profiles on the top surface of the sea, and a small gap at the back where the whale's tail would slot in. Using a jigsaw, I cut out the lower profile of the tail and the gap leading into it from the top, then, simply following the top profile line, carved through to meet the edge of the lower cut. Using a $^5/_{16}$in, 8mm No. 8 gouge, I then cut in the lower point where the dorsal fin would protrude. Now I could slot in the whale and, with a slight adjustment here and there, it fitted very well.

I carved the detail of the splash with a v-tool and $^3/_{16}$in, 5mm No. 3 gouge, then sanded all areas with the five grits. Two coats of sanding sealer were applied, the first rubbed down with 500 grit, the second with 0000 wire wool. A few applications of wax on top combined to give a wonderful finish.

A glass stand seemed the only option to give a good, clear visual effect and I found a remarkably helpful company called Glaze for Trade, who were only too pleased to help design and make the stand for me. ∎

Lee Dickenson has been a self-employed carver for eight years and has undertaken a wide range of carving and sculptural commissions, architectural work, furniture and restoration.

He now has work in private collections all over the UK, as well as in Europe, the USA and as far afield as India. His numerous awards include the Bronze, Silver and Gold Medals at National Woodworker Competitions.

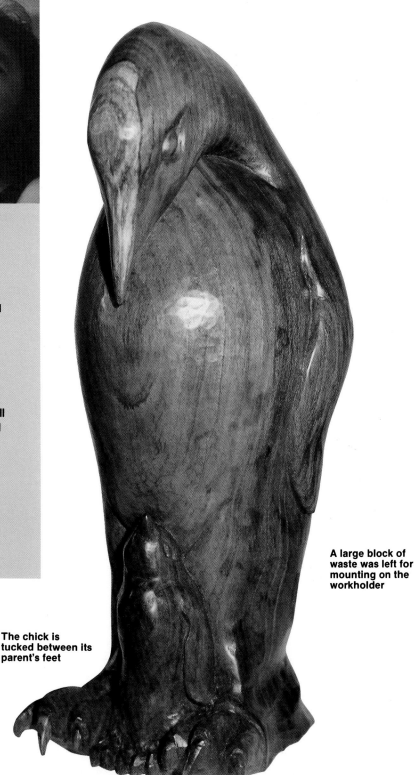

The chick is tucked between its parent's feet

A large block of waste was left for mounting on the workholder

The penguin and its young have been used to symbolise the helpless creatures that inhabit the South Polar region. Seemingly pathetic on land, its only defence is to wobble and slide to the sea. The base my penguin stands on depicts rock and ice and has been arbitrarily joined, showing lines that represent the rest of the world carving up the region.

Let's hope the penguin and all the other creatures are not forced to abandon ship. Although they are at home in that element they cannot survive in it alone.

The penguin was carved from laburnum and the base from walnut (*Juglans regia*). I chose laburnum for its dark colour; the piece seen here actually had a light area of sapwood running down the front, not exactly corresponding with a real penguin's markings but it does suggest the right colours.

The walnut has no special relevance, they were off-cuts from another project. They suggested to me the visible lines of division when I tried to lay out the pieces to see what I had.

The piece of laburnum I had was a quarter-sawn portion of a log. However, the heartwood was not good, with some rot (probably the reason for its felling) and shakes. By the time I had cleaned this away the heartwood more resembled the outer shape of the log! This forced me to choose the sapwood as the front of the bird.

With a drawing already prepared I found that the dimensions of the timber I had left would not allow me to square the block on

PENGUIN IN PERIL

LEE DICKENSON WANTED HIS PENGUIN TO CONVEY HIS CONCERN ABOUT THE ANTARCTIC

sort of skittle shape. I have a tendency, in moments of excitement, to get carried away. It would have been easy to just flatten off the corners, forgetting to shape and round the body (practice on scrap pieces might help).

When I had got well into the rounding process it became clear that my drawings were wrong! The shape and position of the wings from the front did not correspond with the side drawing. Luckily I had positioned the wings from the side drawing, giving my desired picture. It could have ruined the carving had it been the other way round.

all sides. I managed the front and two sides but the back had to be left rounded. This was a little disconcerting as I know from experience that accurately band-sawing irregularly shaped blocks is not that easy, or safe. A jig is needed to support blocks like this, to stop them being dragged over by the blade with the possibility of dragging fingers with them.

For marking out, all I needed was a ruler, dividers and a clear marker pen. The drawing for the front was easily transferred but part of the side drawing had to be filled in freehand. The shape of the penguin makes this an easy carving as it is mostly a wasting job with few details to complicate. The adult's head outline, sides of legs and wings were drawn on first, followed by the chick's outline.

The block could be held in a vice for carving, either by the body or preferably by a base. I used the latter method first, then later on secured the base to a hydraclamp workholder. However, the whole carving could have been completed in the vice. It is wise to allow for a solid base; laburnum is a hard timber, using gouges and a mallet the holding system has to take quite a pounding.

First cuts were made with a v-tool to clear a line. A large gouge was then used to chop across to relieve the chick's and adult's heads. A smaller gouge was used to chop round the outline of the chick, and subsequent cross-cutting cleaned the front of the adult either side of the chick. The

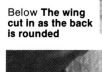

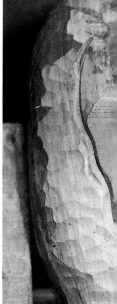

Below **The wing
cut in as the back
is rounded**

v-tool was employed to clean the form of the adult's head.

The body

When coming to carve the adult's body it needed a little thought. What I wanted to achieve was a

**Starting to round
the front of the
body with a large
gouge**

Getting over that little hurdle reminded me that we have the ability to help ourselves, whereas some other creatures of this planet don't.

After rounding, the wings were defined and the neck crease brought on round to match. Then I began shaping the back, in the

As the body is rounded the wings and the neck crease are defined

The chick is carved as the feet are defined

same way as the front.

As carving progressed the wing was given a little form and the head began to be shaped. Again a rounding technique is needed for these tasks, the only difference is the tool; after initial work with a small gouge I finished off with a flat chisel.

Shaping the head, the hollow where beak joins head is marked

My attention then turned to the chick nestled between its parent's feet. The waste removal in this part is the most fiddly, however using the v-tool to mark, then a small gouge to chop out the waste, it is not that hard.

As more definition is achieved around the adult's toes so more details can be mapped out on the chick.

The chick's body becomes more recognisable and the adult's toes can be modelled to match. Study of the drawings and photographs is needed to see the detail of the toes. The divisions between the adult's toes were cut in with a small v-tool and the sides pared down where necessary with a small chisel. A little care was needed in this area as the adult's toes are raised and after undercutting they have little support.

As the chick takes shape the body of the parent is modelled to accept its offspring and the tail is also shaped.

Returning to the head, the eyes were marked in. These were formed by punching in gouges around the drawn on eye, then cutting in to that line from the outside to form a 'moat'. The eyeball was shaped by turning the gouge over and rounding down the sides. A little definition was given to the eye at either end

with a small-tool and the surrounding area rounded down.

After giving the whole thing a going over, cleaning up obvious marks, I decided to give it a coat of linseed oil to show up any other marks. The whole thing was then worked over and over, gradually cleaning up. Any nasty grain was sorted out with a suitably shaped riffler rasp, then rubbed over with abrasive papers to give a smooth surface. I left small tool marks where I thought that they helped to define or portray detail.

The temporary base was cut off and the underside of the adult bird and its toes were finished off, then it was set aside for mounting.

A coat of shellac shows up rough patches to be worked on

Before final mounting the base had to be bleached to give it the ice and rock effect I wanted. This was done by freely painting the bleach on the top but not worrying too much about the sides. After the action of the bleach this left a covering of 'ice' with the timber colour below representing the rock.

First try of the penguin on the base mounting

Clamping the base for gluing

The mount

The irregular shape of the pieces forming the base mounting presented some problems, as they were difficult to hold when clamping up.

When I decided what was going where, the edges were planed and cross-hatched to aid bonding. I joined two side pieces together first and, with a large selection of clamps to apply pressure from all directions, the two halves were joined.

Once I had finally decided where the penguin was to be sited on the base, it was a simple operation to mark out and drill through the mount to secure the body with a few screws.

I finished the penguin with shellac before fixing it to the base, so as not to risk spilling any on the ice. After a couple of coats of shellac had dried, I rubbed down with some wax and fine wire wool, and a final rub with a duster made it shine. ∎

Penguin standing on icy rock with its chick at its feet

Chris Manley was born in 1948 and has lived most of his life in Wareham, Dorset, though his career as a trout farmer also led him to work in Scotland, Gloucestershire and most recently for three years in Northern Ireland.

An enthusiasm for the beauty of wood was kindled through turning at school, and Chris always promised himself a lathe one day, but instead finally took up woodcarving, of the saw and rasp variety, in 1991. His wife politely accepted a wooden heron for a Christmas present and the work took off from there.

He was fortunate in finding people kept wanting to buy the carvings he produced, and found that commissions were beginning to come in. He successfully applied to the Dorset TEC for an Enterprise Allowance and now works full time at home carving wildlife subjects.

Chris has a BTEC Graphics Diploma in Natural History Illustration gained in 1986 after a two-year sabbatical from the trout industry.

He lives in a converted barn with his wife and two children (the critics!) plus a pointer, two Abbyssinian cats and a pen of noisy wildfowl.

Barn owl and 150-year-old hornbeam

POWER CARVING

Chris Manley

Carving natural subjects does not have to be done with traditional hand tools. Chris shows how he makes his carvings with flexible drive cutters and flap wheel sanders.

The hornbeam tree shown here is one in a row planted around 1837 when Queen Victoria came to the throne as a girl, according to the records of the estate where I am lucky enough to live. The row is now gappy and nearing the end of its life, but provides some fine and interesting timber for my woodstore. The barn owl is made from it.

I use a Moviluty flexible drive machine with tungsten carbide cutters (burrs) for all my indoor work. The cutters turn at 24,000 RPM so are excellent for removing wood smoothly and steadily.

There is plenty of time for keeping control of the whole shape. Since you can safely hold the work in one hand while cutting with the other, you can move the carving around as you work which helps keep the proportions relative.

In spite of the high speed of the cutters they are very safe to use. I've never done myself an injury, though I do wear a leather glove to support thin work in my hand such as the wings of the tern, especially when removing the final layers.

A project starts with a strong simple design — something with a distinctive shape that will let the markings in the wood show through.

Burrs are very good for producing well contoured shapes but not so suitable for crisp details in the manner of traditional woodcarving, which needs to be borne in mind.

The subject should be recognisable but a fair amount of artistic licence seems to be quite acceptable (luckily!). Slightly exaggerating the distinctive feature of the subject does no harm either and it tends to happen anyway.

To some extent I try to match the features of the timber to the feel of the subject. The flowing lines of yew go with the swimming otter, and the white sapwood gives the eel its pale underside. The light hornbeam resembles the white plumage of the hovering tern, and the contrasts in the spalted beech (a log from my neighbour's log pile) go with the stilt in as much as it is a black and white bird. I couldn't resist adding the nest and mottled eggs when I started cutting in to the log.

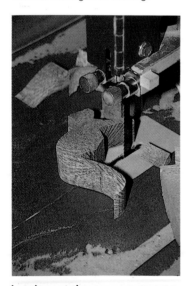

Leaping cat shape cut out on the bandsaw

A friend nearby has a cork tree which provided the interesting variegated patterns for the cat and the curlew, and I hoped the plane tree markings might look like salmon scales. However, it's always exciting seeing what comes out of the wood, and it is never quite what you expect. This is half the fun of a natural material.

Having settled on a rough design idea the next step is to choose a piece of timber. Hopefully my indoor store will provide a suitable stable, seasoned piece of wood that will not shake or show cracks when being carved.

Logs I have brought indoors and cut up I often mark with weights and dates so I can see if they are still losing moisture and liable to be unstable. But even bought timber can give problems when being worked, so there is no guarantee. Keeping work-in-progress in a polythene bag helps to stop cracks appearing overnight.

The size of the selected piece of timber will determine the dimensions of the carving. It is helpful to do several drawings of a subject from various angles using whatever references are to hand, ideally from life but anything can be useful.

These drawings are purely for my own benefit and help familiarise me with distinctive shapes and attitudes. No one else is going to see them and they certainly wouldn't win any illustration prizes! Wood is such interesting material in itself that lots of exact detail can detract from its beauty. I'm after a lively and recognisable form that shows off the timber as well.

Using a soft pencil or crayon I'll next try to sketch my idea onto the wood itself and rough it out on the bandsaw from one viewpoint, then more sketching and sawing from the other side. It adds a bit of life to a carving (and stops it looking too 'wooden'!) to incorporate at least one part asymmetrical.

Working on the cat with the flexidrive

I might turn a head slightly away from the body line as with the curlew and stilt. A salmon keeps on swimming even when it is airborne so my fish viewed from above has a slight S curve to his body.

I've learned not to try to get too close to the final shape with the saw to allow a bit for the 'Oops!'

Otter sketch, mount and block of yew

Bandsawn otter with oak root mount

Photo by Bob Richardson. All other photos by Chris Manley

Just past the "It'll never work" stage

factor when actually carving, but you can certainly trim off a lot of corners and so forth on the bandsaw, as long as the work is well supported.

After sawing, the initial shaping is usually done with the largest D-ended burr, working down the sizes as the work becomes more defined. I seem to use three or

Salmon starter kit

perhaps four different cutters for each piece.

I still nearly always have a point at which I feel the carving is never going to work, usually when it is a smoothed but not detailed lump. I almost gave up on the salmon at one point and in fact went as far as to cut out a new design on the bandsaw before giving myself a severe talking-to.

If it is not finished then no one is going to buy it. All that time and effort already spent will be wasted, and anyway no one else knows what it should look like. If my whale comes out as a sardine then who is to know? Besides all that, I do not like being defeated by what is, after all, only a piece of wood.

I like my work to be smoothly finished with contours rather than details, though I usually indicate eyes. Most of the smoothing can be done with flap wheel sanders — medium 80 and fine 240. These work best at slow speed, especially the fine.

A useful tip given me by another flexidrive user to reduce burning is to remove alternate flaps with pliers. The whole carving is then thoroughly rubbed with fine 360 emery, two coats of Briwax sanding sealer applied, rubbed down with the 360 then 800 emery and polished with two coats of Briwax paste wax.

Most carvings need a base or groundwork of some sort and the waders of course need legs. For these I use well-weathered galvanised fencing wire, unpainted as I feel it tones well with wood.

Sometimes the base will be made from the same timber for continuity, rather like using a limited palette in a painting, or it may be integral like the salmon, or perhaps the carving was designed

with a particular mount in mind as was the otter. Other times I have to think and experiment.

For the tern the original plan was to use a piece of the same hornbeam with a nice wavy grain that might suggest the sea, but that turned out to look a bit dull and the support wire (part of a coathanger) was too obvious.

The piece of oak burr with swirly marks could be interpreted as rough water, and being dark seemed to lift the carving without showing the wire. It's all part of the composition and purely personal but can contribute greatly to the whole picture.

"Will this fish ever come right?"

Originally the salmon base came out as far as his jaw, but I felt it was far more lively with the fish leaping beyond the base so I lopped a few inches. A good stout mount reduces the chance of the carving being knocked over. The curlew on his stone from nearby Kimmeridge beach is very stable and also appropriate as curlews spend a lot of time on beaches.

Before waxing the base I mark it with details of the subject (in case of doubt over what I've actually been trying to carve), the wood and perhaps where it came from, if known, sign it and that's it.

You can then relax and admire the new piece all finished and gleaming away from the dust and clutter of the workshop, wonder why you thought it would never come right, and get all keen to start a new design and another piece of timber. Woodcarving is addictive! ■

Moviluty flexible drive machines, tungsten carbide burrs and flap wheel sanders are all available from: Hegner UK, Unit 8, North Crescent, Diplocks Way, Hailsham, E. Sussex BN27 3JF. Tel: 0323 442440.

BLACK-TAILED

DESIREE HAJNY

Desiree Hajny's interest in woodcarving began when she taught art for six years in a small Nebraska cattle-ranching community. Today she is regarded by many as America's finest animal carver. The first prize she was awarded in the Painted Realistic Animal Class in the 1992 International Woodcarvers competition, is the latest of numerous major awards she has won since 1989.

Carving

Trace the full-sized pattern onto a 4" x 3" x 3" 100mm x 75mm x 75mm high piece of wood with the grain running horizontally. Begin carving by removing the excess wood until your rough has the curves and contours shown in the drawings and photographs.

The face is important. Draw the centreline. If you want the head turned, move the centreline over left or right. (Remember the beginning of the centreline from the top of the head should be over the area where the neck is connected to the skull; marked on top view with a circle.)

From the centreline, measure out the distance between the edges of the nose — ¼" 6mm or about the width of a pencil. It flairs up as it goes to the face. The eye socket is located about a pencil width from the centreline. This is the hollow where the eyeball, the eyelid and muscles that operate the eye are located.

The eyes are towards the top of the head (to 1/3 part) for protection while the animals are eating. They see over their food. The eyes are located on the side of the head so that predators can be watched for from either direction. The muzzle is the width of the middle of the eyeballs (three pencil widths).

The checks, or jaw area are five pencil widths (1¼" 32mm). They are wider than the edge of eyes (from front view).

Trim the excess wood from the top. For the nose, cleft and mouth, V-cut along the pencil line, using the pattern as a reference.

For the eyes, cut a V-shape for the upper and lower lid. Make an

Prairie Dog. Taken in Tucson, Arizona, by Dave Stetson

Surface lines to show planes of the face and body. (Texture too.)

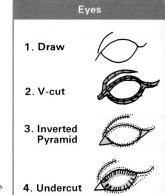

Eyes

1. Draw

2. V-cut

3. Inverted Pyramid

4. Undercut

KEY:		
		V-cut (V-parting tool)
		Undercut (knives, chisels, gouges)
		Inverted pyramid (knife point)
		Hollow out (gouge, veiner . . .)
		Round out (knives, chisels, gouges)

PRAIRIE DOG

Carved side.
Photo Bob
Mischka

Front view.
Half carved, half
burned. Photo
Bob Mischka

**Woodburned
side.** Photo Bob
Mischka

inverted pyramid at the tear-duct. Outline the eyeball with curving stop-cuts. Round out the eyeball.

When the ears are drawn, V-cut or veiner out the outside of the ear (not where cartilage connects to the skull). Hollow out leaving the roll of edge out. Notice that the ears are tucked close to the head for protection from dirt when the prairie dogs are passing through their tunnels. You can't see the ears from the front view.

If you are doing the front feet, there are four longer toes with claws and one short inside toe also with a claw. Carve the shape of the foot. Space the toes with equally spaced V-cuts. Shape up each toe with a V-cut or knife.

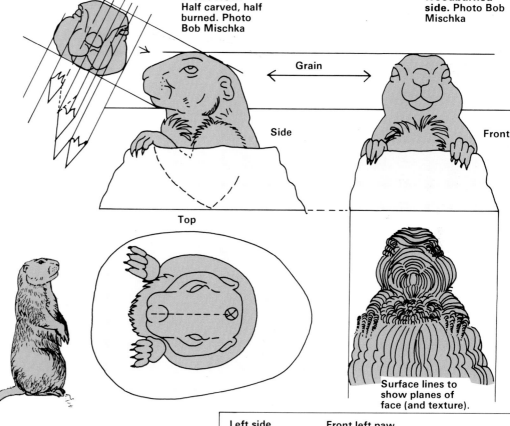

Grain

Side

Front

Top

Surface lines to
show planes of
face (and texture).

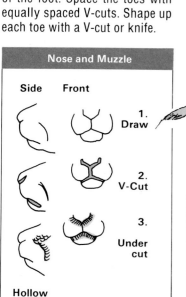

Nose and Muzzle

Side	Front	
		1. Draw
		2. V-Cut
		3. Under cut
Hollow		

Ears

Draw	cartilage connects		
	V-Cut	Hollow out	Hair direction

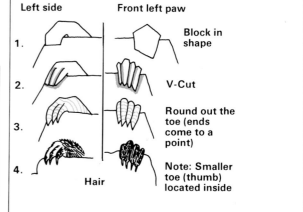

Left side	Front left paw	
1.		Block in shape
2.		V-Cut
3.		Round out the toe (ends come to a point)
4. Hair		Note: Smaller toe (thumb) located inside

Hair-Tract for the Woodburner (adjustable thermostat)

Woodburning

Make small marks in layers using the hair tract as a guide. An adjustable woodburner (one with a thermostat), is recommended for best results. Any tip that comes to a point will help with small hairs on the face.

Use a fluid motion and avoid putting in too many straight lines. Remember the gravity pulls the fur. The fur flows over the head following contours.

Sketches may be used as a reference for burned in, or painted on, marks.

To obtain shiny eyes, sear the wood of the eyeball with the side of a hot-burning tip. It will seal the wood as it darkens it. The final finish will sit on top of the seared areas and they will glisten. Sear the claws also.

Painting

Whatever type of paint you choose, keep it thinned so the pigment doesn't clog up burn marks or carving details.

You want wood colour to show through. Let the colours bleed into one another. Start with light colours first and gradually paint with darker ones until you've hit the darkest. Let these colours dry completely. Use up the colours left on the palette. This way the colours will blend with the animal. Mammals are usually coloured to blend in with their habitat.

Dry-brush areas with lighter colours. This sets off areas the sun would be hitting.

When the brush has just a hint of colour in the bristles, colour only the high points — dull whites and tans. Dry-brush on the base also.

Use a detail round brush to paint black on the eyes and claws. Clean the brush and put a tiny point of white on the top of the eye where the sun would hit the eyeball.

After the paint dries, apply a clear finish. ∎

Angle from back

Three-quarter view — side

Front

Recommended Tools for Prairie Dog
8mm V-parting; 4mm No. 8 gouge; 1mm No. 11 veiner; 8mm No. 3 Fishtail gouge; Carver's eye punch ⅛ (or use detail knife).

Adjustable Burner
Different types:
Detail Master; Nibs Burner; Nibs; Detailer; Multi Max.
Any point that comes to a point 2D Point

Paint Brushes
White Bristle Flat; Stiff Bristle size 3-9/32 width; Small Point — pointer or liner; Size 8 Stable round.

All available from: WOODCRAFT, 210 Wood County Industrial Park, PO Box 1686, Parkersburg, W. Virginia 26102-1686, USA.
Ph. 1-800-225-1153 for free catalogue.

Different Available Blanks:
Rossiter Ruff-Outs, 1447 S. Santa Fe, Wichita, Kansas 67211, USA.
Ph. 1-800-825-2657 for catalogue.

UK SUPPLIERS
Woodcarving tools:
Ashley Iles (Edge Tools) Ltd, East Kirby, Spilsby, Lincolnshire PE23 4DD.
Tel: (07903) 372.

Stuart R. Stevenson, Artists and Gilding Materials, 68 Clerkenwell Road, London EC1M 5QA.
Tel: (071) 253 1693.

Henry Taylor Tools Ltd, The Forge, Lowther Road, Sheffield S6 2DR.
Tel: (0742) 340282.

Adjustable Burners:
Pintail Supplies, 20 Sheppenhall Grove, Aston, Nantwich, Cheshire CW5 8DF.
Tel: (0270) 780056.

Paint Brushes
E. Ploton (Sundries) Ltd, 273 Archway Road, London N6 5AA.

Also Stuart R. Stevenson.

A STORY OF DECOY WILDFOWL

CLIFF BENTON

Modern decoy bird carving grew from hunting equipment developed in North America.

Cliff Benton, B.A., Dip.C.D. Ex-Chairman of British Decoy Wildfowl Carving Association. Retired teacher-training lecturer, Cliff spent nine years on the staff at Dundee College of Education and two years at Kericho Teachers' College in Kenya. He has written articles for woodcraft magazines, both in Britain and in New Zealand.

His interest in decoys began with a visit to the Shelburne Museum in Vermont USA and a hands-on course with the late Bob Ridges of Farrington Gurney, Avon in 1984. Later courses have been with nationally-known American carvers, Mark McNair of Virginia, Bill Porterfield of Pennsylvania, Jim Sprankle of Maryland and most recently Jan Fitch of Kingston, Ontario.

Presently, he is working on a pair of shelduck, half-size mallards and various commissions. He was responsible for organising the British Wildfowl Art Festival in 1990 and repeated this event in June 1993.

Wooden decoys play a part in American history stretching back to the earliest settlers. If their history is short their interest in what they have is long. Some years ago on a visit to New England, I chanced on a museum of early settlers' artifacts, such as only the Americans could produce.

The Shelburne Collection was started by a wealthy New York couple, and has a miscellany of everyday objects, from weapons to tools and farm implements, and many examples of early transportation. Most of the collection is held in reconstructed log cabins and barns. Imagine my surprise and delight on entering one of these buildings to find it devoted to decoy ducks and wildfowling memorabilia. Here were hundreds of old decoys with the names of revered craftsmen, who had not only made them but hunted over them.

Even before the arrival of the Europeans, the native American tribes hunted in the lakes and forests where wildlife abounded. Hunting with bow and arrow and fishing were their means of survival. Wildfowl were numerous, the flight paths of duck and geese crisscrossing the country from South

The origins of duck decoys, made of rush covered with feathers by the native peoples of North America. Courtesy of the Museum of the American Indian, Heye Foundation, New York

to North in annual migration. In the West the Indian is known to have used decoys — bundles of rushes and dried skins and feathers fashioned into the shape of resting birds. When the settlers came they too had to hunt to eat, using guns. They quickly followed the Indian ways and began to make decoys in wood.

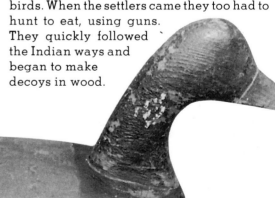

A Brant Goose by the late Baird Carter of Delaware, a gifted amateur

The essence of successful decoys is their ability to attract flying wildfowl; but the hunter making his own decoys had to consider both floating properties and durability. The early carvers used axes to rough hew the bodies and heads, before detailing the head and back feathers to some semblance of the living bird with a sharp tool such as a Bowie knife. Today old decoys turn up from time to time, to be identified or argued

A Canvasback Duck by James T. Holly of Chesapeake Bay, about 1890; typical of a hunters' decoy of the time

about, as the work of certain craftsmen from this or that specific area of the States. Some of these old pieces, looking very sad after years of use on the water, can fetch very high prices from collectors.

On my first visit to New Orleans, the centre of the Louisiana Wildfowl Carvers and Collectors Guild, still searching for the origins of the great interest in these objects to be found all over North America, I came on an exhibition, 'Art from the Wild'. Hand-carved decoys and lifelike interpretations were on display among paintings and taxidermy. Here I found carvers anxious to talk about their work.

The difference between the reproduced old decoys and the new decorative birds was astonishing, exactness of detail extending to individual feathers. I also visited 'Sports Art' shops and was told of the two true folk-arts originating in New Orleans, decoy making and jazz. The former largely brought to the area by the Cajuns (religious persecuted 'Arcadians' from the far North) and the latter stemming from the Negro slaves.

Overhunting and conservation

In the 19th century duck hunting was widespread and destructive; huge shoots downing birds in their thousands were decimating the wildfowl population. Battery shooting was carried out from half-sunken punts trailing scores of decoys, ending the day with hundreds of birds killed for the growing markets of restaurants in the

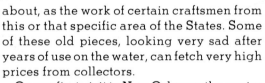

Mitchel La France at 90 was still chopping traditional working decoys, and they are now collectors' items. The wood is Cyprus root

Over a long career of carving decoys Mitchel La France wore out several pocket knives like this one

Eastern cities. Eventually the authorities, both federal and State, had to clamp down. Early in the present century growing concern, mainly from sportsmen, for conservation of wildlife led to the formation of an association known as 'Ducks Unlimited'. It was they who, in the 1920's and during the Depression, organised work, with the help of farmers both in US and Canada, to save, protect and improve the breeding grounds in the North.

Today, all over the States, there are parklands set up for the still flourishing sport of duck hunting, now carefully controlled as to season and 'bag' per person. In the post-war years returning servicemen increased the sporting fraternity and many began to make their own decoys. From this renewed interest has evolved, using increasingly specialised machine tools and modern acrylic paints, the new art form – decorative decoy making. Birds such as mallard, teal, pochard and the pintail are made in a variety of woods; basswood (*Tilia Americana*), similar to European lime (*Tilia vulgaris*), and tupelo (*Nyssa aquatica*) being the most commonly used. In Britain jelutong (*Dyera costulata*) and lime, or imported sugar pine (*Pinus Lambertiana*) are the woods in use.

Decorative birds, as opposed to hunting decoys, show extra realism, particularly in the texturing or feathering detail, and the use of a natural-looking paint finish with several layers of colour washes. They are often mounted in natural-looking foliage or on rocks (made from the same wood). Encouraging this art-form are a range of clubs and associations which hold annual

A pair of Wood Duck by Benjamin Schmitt of Michigan, rare collector's pieces

A Mason Mallard (snaky head), stamped 'Premier Grade' on the base

A Ruddy Duck drake carved by Bill Birk of Bridgeport, Connecticut. A winner at the Atlantic Flyaway contest. Bill Birk pioneered realism in decoy carving

competitions, awarding certificates and titles as well as large money prizes.

The competition is fierce and the quality of the exhibits has steadily become more and more sensational. The most prestigious of these shows is the Ward Foundation Wildfowl Carving and Art Exhibition, held annually in Maryland. The title is taken from the Ward brothers, barbers, whose seasonal sideline was decoy making.

At such events world champions are created and among names is that of Tan Brunet, known as 'the Cajun carver'. He is a fourth generation decoy maker with sons following him into competitions and winning awards. He, and many others use tupelo gum, the root wood of a Louisiana swamp plant. Using wet wood and traditional tools (axe and Bowie knife) and painting in the local tradition of oil paints, they produce their work and enter it in championship class contests.

Another famed carver, Charles Hutchinson, has a set piece of a pair of Bald Eagles fighting over a fish, on permanent exhibition in the Kentucky State capital building. It was purchased, before being presented to the State, for US$24,000. ∎

BLACK-FOOTED FE

DESIREE HAJNY

Desiree Hajny's interest in woodcarving began when she taught art for six years in a small Nebraska cattle-ranching community. Today she is regarded by many as America's finest animal carver. The first prize she was awarded in the Painted Realistic Animal Class in last year's International Woodcarvers competition is the latest of numerous major awards she has won since 1989.

Begin by tracing the full-size pattern on to a 6½" x 3" x 2½" 165mm x 75mm x 63mm piece of wood with the grain running vertically. Cut out on a bandsaw.

Remove excess wood until your rough has the curves and contours in the drawings and photographs. If you prefer a blank, an address is available at the end with details.

The face is important. Draw the centreline from the top of the nose to between the ears. The centreline goes down the centre of the skull to where the neck connects to it, (marked on top view with a circle).

After trimming the excess wood on the head from the top view and front view, centre the pencil on centreline (FIG 1). It's approximately the width of the nose pad, (pad is smaller). It hits around the

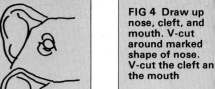

FIG 2 Surface texture

Head 1

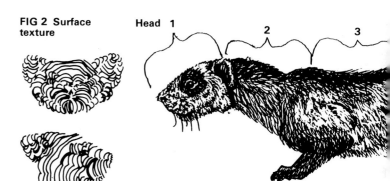

EYES

FIG 3 Eye —Draw up eye and lid

1. Stop cut or V-cut around the eye shape and tear duct, brow and the eye-lid

2. Inverted pyramid by the tear duct and undercut behind the eye of the temple area

3. Undercut eyeball

4. Sear the eyeball with edges of burner point

NOSE AND MOU

FIG 4 Draw up nose, cleft, and mouth. V-cut around marked shape of nose. V-cut the cleft an the mouth

Undercut

Gouge out nostri

Sear the nose wi edges of burner point

Closer to nose

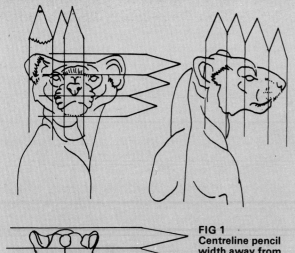

FIG 1 Centreline pencil width away from centre measure hits outside of muzzle — point of cartilage nearest to centreline of ear

Back of eye is two pencil widths away from tip of nose. Four pencil widths nose to middle of ear

EARS

FIG 5 Ear — Draw up shape of ear. Mark in cartilage roll, and the hollow

1. Shape up the back of the ear

2. Hollow out the inside leaving outside roll

3. Texture inside of ear

4. Woodburn edges using the hair tract available to follow direction of short strokes

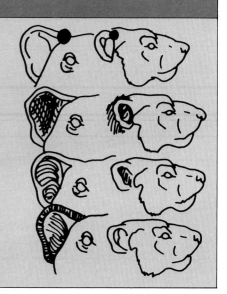

RRET

Hair tract

5

Six head lengths long

One and one-third head lengths tall

chin width, (chin is a little wider), and the inside of the eye socket.

The surface texture will let you plane out your face, (FIG 2). Measure a pencil width from the centreline, (FIG 1). Notice how this line hits the outside part of the eye socket and width of the muzzle. It also measures the top connecting part of the ear.

This socket is hollow where the eyeball, eye lid, and muscles that operate the eye are located. From the front view the head is four pencil widths. Using the charts, (FIGS 3, 4 and 5) follow the directions on each part of the face, eye, nose, and ears.

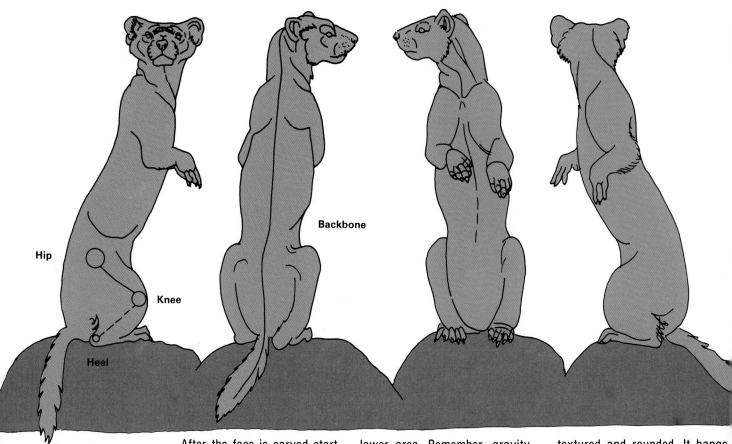

Hip

Knee

Heel

Backbone

After the face is carved start concentrating on the front legs. They are hanging from the body. Shape up this area referring to the pattern. The shoulders and scapula are tapered toward the spine, marked by the centreline. Use a gouge to sink this in.

The stomach area also tapers from the spine. It is rounded toward the bottom. Texture the lower area. Remember, gravity will pull the skin downward making the tummy bulge slightly.

The pelvis area tapers just slightly from the spine. The hip will bulge out as marked on the pattern. The knee will stick out. Then fold back in the lower leg, knee to heel.

Using FIG 6 continue shaping the lower legs and feet. The tail is textured and rounded. It hangs down. Check over the ferret comparing it to the pattern.

Woodburning

Make small layers by using marks referring to the hair tract as a guide. An adjustable woodburner, (one with a thermostat),

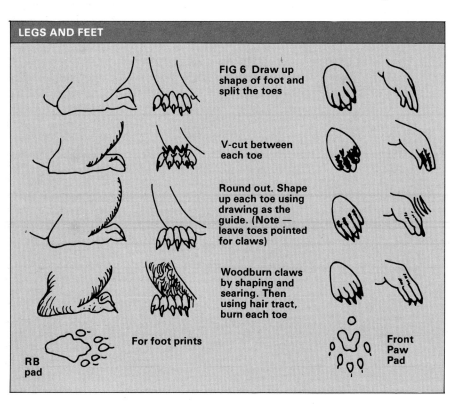

LEGS AND FEET

FIG 6 Draw up shape of foot and split the toes

V-cut between each toe

Round out. Shape up each toe using drawing as the guide. (Note — leave toes pointed for claws)

Woodburn claws by shaping and searing. Then using hair tract, burn each toe

For foot prints

RB pad

Front Paw Pad

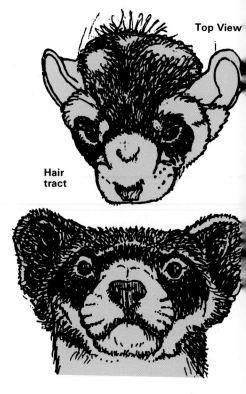

Top View

Hair tract

is recommended for best results. Any tip that comes to a point will help with small hairs on the face, (with the exception of the writing tip).

Use a fluid 'stab-pull' motion. Avoid putting too many straight lines. Gravity pulls the fur. The fur follows the contours of animal planes.

For heavy textured areas pull the burner tip deep across and along the deep areas of veiner or V-cut. Then pull the burner tip from one deep area up over the high points and end up in another deep part of the ravine, (made by a V-cut or veiner).

To obtain shiny eyes sear the wood of the eyeball with the side of a hot burning tip. It will seal the wood as it darkens it. The final finish will sit on top of the seared areas and they will glisten.

Sear the claws and nose pad. For the white spots and white areas simply turn down the heat on the burner.

A hint to help — mark in areas that are lighter with a pencil and draw in the direction of the fur. This serves as a guideline.

The carving half burned

Painting

Whatever type of paint you choose, keep it thinned so the pigment doesn't clog up the texture worked in by the burner.

It is desirable to have the wood colour showing through. Let the colours bleed together, (get pictures of a ferret that show what colours you will need).

Start with light colours and gradually work into the darker ones until you've hit black. Let these colours dry completely. Use up the colours left on the palette completely on the base. This way the colours will work with the animal. Mammals have colours that blend in with their habitat.

Drybrush areas on the animal to set off texture and to show where the sun is hitting the ferret. (Drybrush — the brush has just a hint of colour in the bristles — colour only high points). Drybrush on base also.

Use a detail round brush to paint the eyes and nose of the ferret. Clean out the brush and put a tiny point of paint on the top of the eye where the sun hits the eyeball. After the paint dries put a clear finish on.

The colouration of the ferret is as follows: lighter tans and buff under the belly, brownish black on the backbone, dark mask around eyes, face white above and below the mask. Keep in mind that each one varies a bit. ■

For those interested in purchasing the carving blank for the project it can be ordered from: Rossiter's Ruffouts, 1447 S. Santa Fe, Wichita, KS 67211, USA.

Cost per blank is $16 (US). This includes shipping and handling. Those interested in seeing their catalogue can send $3. This will be refunded on first order. Those ordering blanks will receive a catalogue.

J udith started carving in 1986 on a week's course run by the late Bob Ridges. Her main occupations then were golf, tennis and embroidery. Now her only activity/ occupation is carving almost obsessively.

During her real working life she has been a secretary, a school teacher and, after studying at London University for her MA and Doctorate, an educational researcher.

Her more advanced training in carving was in America with world champion Jim Sprankle. She has exhibited over there at the prestigious Easton Waterfowl Festival, Maryland, and tries to visit each year for courses or shows. Her ambition is to improve her detailed carvings and to learn to paint them in oils.

Her work is in several styles as there is no type of bird carving that does not interest her. Constant experimenting with hollow decoys, textured and natural finishes, types of paint and stains and different woods keeps her adaptable and inventive. She has moved on this last year to carving birds of prey and songbirds.

She puts her progress down to natural doggedness, hard work and the helpfulness of every other carver she knows.

DAVID TIPPEY
Stylised Black-Winged Stilt

PHILIP NELSON
Mallard and chick, decorative style. Lime/acrylics, 1991

JUDITH NICOLL

All you need is a knife, strips of sandpaper and a sense of adventure.

T he growing number of decoy carvers in recent years, and the subsequent development of some of these carvers into fully-fledged detailed bird carvers, has been astonishing.

There are those who carve the traditional hollowed and weighted floating duck decoys. Others have progressed into carving ducks in breathtaking realistic style — and then extended their range to cover birds of prey, or songbirds. Finally there are all those who carve birds in different woods with a natural finish, adapting their designs to bring out the natural beauty of the wood figuring as would any wood carver.

The most popular form of bird carving, under the collective term of 'decoy carving', is the detailed or decorative style with feathers etched in and painted. Ian Norbury summed up the initial

GETTING STARTED AS A DECOY CARVER

reaction to these carvings when he called them a 'bit of a mystery to other carvers, if not for the how then for the why'. An attempted explanation is the reason for this article.

Floating Sculpture

Most of the enthusiasm for the ancient traditional form of decoy carving was spread in the UK by the late Bob Ridges. He took up carving after discovering decoys in New Orleans in 1980. By the mid-80s he had set up a school of decoy carving and introduced hundreds of people to the charms of 'floating sculpture'.

This is the term coined by Joel Barber who published the first book on Wild Fowl Decoys in 1934 in the USA. A New York architect, he was considered the first major collector to also build up a correlated history of the development of the decoy. He was a romanticist and brought an awareness to the Americans of the importance and value of their own folk culture.

Decoys' sometimes crude shapes have the classic elegance and appeal of the working artefact with understated beauty and clean lines. These utilitarian objects are now collected and carved as ornaments but their history and the men who carved and hunted with them adds to their romance.

The names are now legends: 'Umbrella' Watson, 'Cigar' Daisey, 'Fresh Air Dick' Jansen —

and the names revered by collectors: the Ward brothers, Shang Wheeler, and Joe Lincoln whose preening Pintail it was that achieved a record $319,000 at auction in 1989. Their folk history has a quality of its own.

The oldest decoys were very crude; some were made of old telegraph poles, butts of poles of white cedar used to grow hops; old railway sleepers, or fence rails with pine knots fashioned for heads. The crude methods of shaping with axes is still used by the Louisiana champions in the early stages of their detailed decorative birds. Certainly many of the large numbers of professional decoy carvers I visited in the States still carve with saw, axe, spokeshave and drawknife.

Sophisticated paint and detail do not necessarily make a good decoy. Characteristic, although crude, decoys which capture the character and essence of the bird will 'draw 'em down good'; bad decoys will spook the hunters' prey.

To take up decoy carving today is to be drawn into the romance and history, into the fascination of the different styles and methods of construction, into the regional differences and characters of the early carvers' work. The large open waters of the northern lakes heavy with pack-ice demanded large stable decoys with a prow; the swamps and bayous of the south called for lifesize, well-painted birds to catch and hold the attention of the live birds against a vivid coloured backdrop. Laws against hunting on Sundays in some States demanded small, hollow and folding decoys to be hurriedly hidden in poachers' pockets.

These differences of the past are part of the attraction for the present-day carver. There is no standard method; no standard style; and lastly, no less-than-shapely bird can rightfully be criticised. Each novice's misshapen bird has its charm. One of Bob's early pupils told me that the best thing about his course was that everybody's duck was as good as another.

JANE BREWER
Great-Spotted
Woodpecker.
Lime/acrylics

TED OXLEY
Kestrel, 1991

JUDITH NICOLL
Oystercatcher

JOHN STRIDE
Canada Goose

Books
An excellent general all-round book: *The Decoy Duck: from Folk Art to Fine Art* by Bob Ridges. A Dragons World Book.
ISBN 1 85028 059

The New Bruce Burk *Game Bird Carving* Winchester Press.
ISBN 0 8329 0439 2.
This covers getting started for beginners to advanced carvers and can be spotted in most professional workshops.

An excellent picture gallery book of old decoys: *The Great Book of Wildfowl Decoys*, General Editor Joe Engers. Thunder Bay Press 1990.
ISBN 0 934429 75 8

Courses attract all kinds of people of all ages. On my last course in the USA there was a neuro-surgeon, an 80 years old couple, a postman, a Marine and an experienced Canadian carver who had already won ribbons at Intermediate level competition. Everyone can learn to carve a duck; experienced carvers can learn new ideas. All that is needed to start is a knife, strips of sandpaper and a sense of adventure. Rows of carefully sharpened chisels are not required nor is a studio. Decoy carvers brook no criticism from self-styled purist traditional carvers: the answer was given to me by the same pupil mentioned above. 'I can do those, but can they do these?'

Variety

Another attraction is the variety of subject. Once you have started to carve birds there is no limit. You can start with a wren and progress to a covey of quail taking-off; try a pair of scissor-tailed flycatchers or a simple, stylised swan. The infinite variety of shape and form in an American competition is mind boggling: Snowy Owls on crusty ice, Peregrines diving and ducks sleeping. One Essex decoy carver told me 'One's work will be unique every time; no-one can copy; this is new and that impresses people. Woodturning and rocking horses have all been done for years; these feathers are new. If you're looking to express yourself, you can do it better in this field.'

Another Essex carver, a novice, told me of two main attractions for new carvers: 'The skills are not under wraps. This is accessible to someone with a knife and time. It is achievable and there is no bottom line.' He also brought up one of the most important features of this line of carving: the huge support industry generated in the States and now growing here. There are hundreds of books with projects and patterns should you need them; there are monthly magazines with advice, contacts and superb photographs. There are legions of duck carvers only too happy to share their techniques and pass on their enthusiasm. There are specialist tool catalogues which also help and teach. There is no limit to your ability. You can push out the boundaries and try anything and learn and grow and explain constantly that No, you never did have any art training.

One man who understands this more than most is David Clews who, an excellent carver himself, finds himself not just supplying tools as part of his business but also liberal information and advice on every aspect of bird carving to literally hundreds of new carvers. The catalogues of the three specialised suppliers in the UK are based on experience of what is really useful. David explains that bird carving links activities that so many people enjoy: the countryside, birds and wood. 'People amaze themselves at what they can do and have an early reward.'

He again emphasises the small requirements of the first-time carver. Like other suppliers, he will provide a beginners kit: a blank with drawing, eyes and strips of abrasive cloth. For example, the cost of a Teal duck kit with eyes would be £16 + P&P. With this might also come much gentle advice and encouragement, if required.

Suppliers become personal friends in this carving medium as they watch your progress and help with your problems. Pauline McGowan runs courses on site with live ducks outside as models; she has devised a book of patterns of UK ducks to wean those addicted to carving from USA pattern books. Sophie Ridges continues her husband's business with courses now run by former pupils and displays and sells the former pupils' work.

Starting

How does one start that first bird? The question most asked is: 'Do you just start with a block of wood?' and the answer is 'Yes'. You might already be able to draw a crude duck and if so you are half-way there. All you need to do next is draw the second profile as from above. With a duck this is usually egg-shaped. If the size of the side and top profile match, you cut them out in cardboard and trace around them onto a block of wood. The head is usually cut separately. This is so you may have the grain running down the bill on a turned head; also you may make different head positions from the same pattern. This wood is then cut along the lines; more easily on a bandsaw. What emerges is duck-shaped and you start to round off the corners.

Let us try a simple shorebird that you have seen in a photograph of the marshes. Trace around it and put it onto paper. Identify your bird and research its measurements: length and width of body. Enlarge your profile drawing until it is correct. Draw around this onto a block of wood which is cut to the body width measurement. Bandasaw it out.

Easier than this: go to one of the excellent courses and enjoy a weekend with fellow experimenters. Or buy a simple and cheap book such as those by Rosalind Leach Daisey, or the jewel amongst carving books 'Game Bird Carving' by Bruce Burk.

There is nothing wrong with using someone else's patterns in this field of carving when you start. Everything is allowed. In market hunting days there was much swopping of decoys and patterns to make a perfect rig for hunting. There was no question of plagiarism. Certain designs fitted certain local conditions; successful decoy designs were passed around small communities. Many UK carvers have sharpened their teeth on Pat Godin's excellent patterns. He has done the work: the measurements and shapes are there. Why re-invent the wheel? Use the patterns available and learn on them if you are not naturally able to see in 3D. It will not be long before you stretch your wings and make your own flights of fancy!

Materials

Most novices start with Jelutong or Sugar Pine, both easily carved with a knife. The detailed work is best done on Jelutong as it has tight grain and no resin. Oil paints can be put straight on to the sanded wood and can give a nice traditional effect — I have used Japan paints, household paints and stains. Acrylic paints are easiest in many ways for the beginner but need a gesso undercoat. ∎

Useful addresses:
(wood, tools, books, paints etc.)
David & Sheila Clews, Pintail Decoy Supplies, 20 Sheppenhall Grove, Aston, Nantwich, Cheshire CW5 8DF. (0270-780056)

Pauline McGowan, Old Hall Decoys, Old Hall Farm, Scole, Diss, Norfolk IP21 4ES.

Sophie Ridges, The Decoy Gallery, Hollow Marsh, Farrington Gurney, Bristol BS18 5TX. (0761-452075)

More specialised bird and fish carvers may wish to contact P. C. English Inc., PO Box 380, Thornburg, VA 22565, USA or Craftwoods, 2101 Greenspring Drive, Timonium, MD 21093, USA. (There might be a small charge for a catalogue owing to expenses)

Information and help will be willingly given by the Secretary of the British Decoy and Wildfowl Carving Association, Judith Nicoll, 18 Ditton Court Road, Westcliff on Sea, Essex SS0 7HG. (0702-432774) on receipt of a SAE please. The Newsletter gives details of USA magazines, courses here and there, tools and books etc.

FAIR

Fairground organ front, carved by Woody White

Woody White specialises in fairground subjects, producing beautifully carved and hand-painted organ fronts and carousel animals for fairground rides. His mythological creatures are exported to Australia, Japan, North America and Europe, and now commissions arrive from many countries. Recently he started to make miniature carved carousel animals for private collectors and he has also diversified into carved domestic furniture – bed-heads and linen chests adorned with his imaginative designs.

Workshops

Woody White operates from two workshops on a farm in the village of Bleadon, not far from Weston-Super-Mare in the West Country of England. He converted his workshops from milking parlours and dairy buildings, working on the buildings while farm animals paraded through them. The Rural Development Commission helped Woody to establish his workshops, advising on planning and business aspects. They also subsidised exhibition costs and included Woody White in a regional television news story, which attracted new clients.

Detail of a decorated blanket chest

Miniature galloper, about 12in, 300mm long, carved by Woody White, painted by Vicki Postlethwaite

BEASTS

The new workshops are a vast improvement because, previously, Woody worked in a wooden shed at the bottom of the garden, making parts for organ fronts. But this building was quickly outgrown. The turning point came when he was commissioned to carve a large fairground organ front which wouldn't fit into his shed.

One of his new workshops is used for timber preparation and accommodates a circular saw, bandsaw and planer/thicknesser, along with wood ready for carving. Money has been saved by buying secondhand machine tools. For example, the bandsaw is fifty years old and the Sagar planer/thicknesser is a little older. The second workshop, some 27 x 17ft, 8 x 5m, is where the creative work is carried out.

A Japanese bear ready for delivery to Australia

Apart from a mobile power drill, the rest of the workshop accommodates four carving benches and a joinery bench. There is also a carpeted area for finished projects.

Woodcarving is Woody White's second career. At school he received considerable encouragement from Alan Greenland, his woodworking teacher, who remained a close friend all his life. Woody cherishes some old tools and woodworking books which eventually were bequeathed to him from Alan Greenland's estate. Woody spent the early part of his working life in plumbing and building, but became disillusioned with building work. During a period of ill-health in 1987 he decided to become self-employed as a woodcarver. He has been busy and happy ever since.

Timber and tools

Woody White is very meticulous about the timber he uses. Concerned about the variable quality of wood in his early days, he decided to procure his own and dry it in kilns, which he designed and built with his son's help. I met him soon after he had taken delivery of three huge 135-year-old lime trees which had blown down on the Montacute estate. He had the trunks sawn to suit the subjects he carves. The planks, mainly 3¼in, 83mm thick, are then air-dried and stored until ready to complete the drying process in the kilns. Air drying reduces the water content from about 60% to around 20-28%; the kiln continues the drying until a moisture content of 12% is obtained. A Protimeter is used with its probe to measure the water content accurately. There is no room for guesswork.

By procuring, sawing and drying his timber, Woody White saves money and he knows that he will have consistent quality material.

Like most woodcarvers, Woody White has a comprehensive collection of carving tools – many of them quite old. Among his favourites are old Addis, Herring and Clark tools.

Photographs by David Askham

Woody White with a galloper, after initial shaping features are outlined with v-tools

A galloper horse for a new carousel, ready for painting

Getting started

The inspiration for new carvings often comes from discussions with customers. Sometimes they send him photographs or drawings which provide the basis for a new subject. Typical examples are a Japanese bear for the Orient, or a mythological fire-breathing dragon for New York. Woody White then produces a set of drawings. If he has to make a number of similar carvings, he makes up a set of hardboard patterns, whereas for a one-off, he makes paper patterns.

Research is very important when tackling a well-known subject such as galloping horses for

Woody White with his first unicorn during roughing

Flora, the first unicorn carved in this style

a fairground ride. Woody White explains: 'There are very traditional designs for fairground horses, in England and America. For example, English horses go round clockwise whereas American gallopers ride anti-clockwise. I've got a good collection of books with detailed pictures of fairground animals and carved woodwork.

'Next I decide how I am going to put the wooden block together. It is simply a matter of enlarging the appropriate picture, perhaps altering it slightly to achieve a desired effect ... perhaps a different mane or face position.

'The drawing shows the shape I want and pencil lines show how the boards are put together. So I've got a rump block and a double belly board to give the curve under the belly. The legs are mortise and tenoned into the panels. The neck is made up of three panels with an extra piece on one side for the mane ... and the head, again, is three pieces and is hollow. If the horses are going on a roundabout, there is a hole at the back of the open mouth so that on a ride, the air can go right through the head, neck and body, leaving through two holes at the bottom. That design point keeps the wood fresh internally.'

Each bit of wood that offends your eye, you cut it off. When nothing more offends, you have finished.

About thirty-five blocks of limewood make up a large animal, like a galloping horse, but each block might consist of two or three pieces. So it could contain up to one hundred separate pieces of wood. It all depends on what wood is available and what size the panels have to be. Surprisingly, it is not important to assemble all the pieces for one figure from one batch of wood as limewood is very stable and evenly grained. Body panels, laminated from several pieces, are cut on the bandsaw into the various shapes. The assembled block is like a three-dimensional jigsaw puzzle.

Learning curve

Around Woody White's workshop are several woodcarvings for the benefit of visitors who want to see samples of his work. Woody's first galloper, made in 1987, still hangs on his wall. 'In the beginning, a showman asked me the price of my gallopers. I didn't have a clue: I'd never made one. So, just two months into the business I had to drop everything else and make a galloper horse. I made it right from scratch: I really had no experience... Then we met James Noyce, who is one of the leading showmen in this country, who knows a great deal about galloper horses. So, I asked him for his criticism and to point out the good and bad features. He did that very well and, for a cup of tea, I learned a great deal. Most important, I learned how much material it consumed and how many hours of work was involved.

'Everything is done by hand and eye: drawing, marking and carving wood. No two pieces are ever the same. These small horses for a juvenile roundabout are all made from identical blocks of wood, but as soon as you start cutting them, each one turns out a little different and each one has its own personality.'

Woody White has another tale about how he solved a specific carving problem. 'Now when I was carving a Neptune organ front, the first one I ever did, I was really concerned about how to get that tough scraggly hair on Neptune's head. It had to be real raggle-taggle hair. I went to bed thinking about this and during the night I had a dream, that was so vivid, that I just couldn't forget it.

'In the dream, I was in a workshop, which I had never seen before, with a man of about my own age who I presumed was my late maternal grandfather, who I never really knew. In his workshop this man showed me exactly how to draw out the hair and how to proceed to cut the hair. When I came down in the morning I tried out the technique he had demonstrated, on that piece of oak, and it worked! It was exactly what I wanted. I could tell you today every detail of every bit of equipment and machinery in that workshop; it was that vivid. I could draw you the face of the man. I needed help and it came to me in a dream.'

Solving problems through dreams is very rare. Most are solved through trial and error: it is all part of the learning process. You cannot beat the dictum: 'Have a go!' Woody holds the view that anyone can learn to carve to a certain degree. 'Members of my classes find their level within the first year.' In order to meet demand, up to ten students attend Woody's Monday evening carving classes which run continuously throughout the year. Each student pays £4.50 for a two-hour training session and his course is over-subscribed.

Woody White has demonstrated the value of consulting experts in the relevant field; not all need be woodcarvers, as Woody found with James Noyce the showman.

A final word from Woody: 'I am often asked how do I carve, or how do you know when to stop? I have a simple reply. All the time you are carving, you are looking at the piece of wood. You are also seeing, in your mind's eye, the finished object. Each little bit of wood that offends your eye, you cut it off. When nothing more offends your eye, you have finished!' ∎

The test piece for the dream-inspired carving of Neptune's head

David Askham trained as a chartered engineer, but now works full time as a researcher, writer and photographer. As well as crafts, he specialises in travel, business, conservation and horticulture

WORKING IN T

BETTY SKIPPER

Paul Albright works in the woods near Akeley, Minnesota.

We saw the wolf first — or was it a coyote? It was crouching on a granite rock at the top of a grassed bank beside Highway 34 at Akeley, Minnesota, USA. A powerful carving, the body curved in menacing watchfulness of its unseen prey. It was somewhat marred by the shiny urethane finish, but with Minnesota winters dipping well below zero, this is essential protection.

A discreet sign — Albright Sculpture — (we'd have missed it, but for the wolf) pointed us up a track and off to the left, where two hot-dog sized dachsunds tried to intimidate us.

Paul Albright was standing in a kind of rustic bandstand, playing discords on a chainsaw. With birch trees all around, it was an idyllic fine-weather workshop. Seeing us, he left his latest project, partly roughed out with chalk-lines and initial cuts, to shake hands.

'I'm a year behind with work.' He told us, cheerfully, but, 'Oh yuh, I've got time to talk, sure. Nice to see people this time of year.'

He'd only set up in full-time business a year ago. Before that, he had studied sculpture and had been carving part-time for six years. Most of his work is commissioned, with satisfied clients passing the word, but some is on sale in local stores.

An al fresco display-board shows photographs of his carvings, and here and there around the property, amongst trees and shrubs, are lifelike bears, bald eagles (the area has the real thing) gulls, Indians and a pioneer woodsman.

Each figure, either wild creature or human, costs around $500 each, according to size, intricacy and whether finished for indoor display, or protected against the elements.

Using elm, cedar, butternut (white walnut), pine and North American poplar (cottonwood), Albright rough shapes with the chainsaw, then uses an electric grinding disc. Fur, feather and other detail is picked out by hand with traditional carving tools. The finish is sometimes enhanced with a judicious touch of stain, but he prefers to let the natural grain weather for effect.

Paul Albright at work in his summer workshop

This wolf stands at the side of the road near Paul Albright's work place

Bald eagle

'Nice place to work', we said.

'Uhuh, the family's close by, too' — waving a hand towards a small house. We'd noticed the toys outside. 'It's good living here. Quiet.' Sniffing the rich damp-leaf smell, gazing at birch and pine, we agreed.

Though most of his work is sited outdoors, Albright doesn't like to carve standing tree-stumps, unless a client insists.

'Eventually, they just split. Frost gets in the wood, or they dry out.' He prefers to work from a block, then mount the finished piece.

He showed us his winter workshop. As yet, it has a fairly uncluttered look, as if he had spent most of the year outside. An almost-finished Indian-brave sculpture dominated the centre.

But we sensed that we had delayed him long enough. As we left, he was already back at work, earmuffed beneath his canopy, making the most of the decent weather, the saw biting its decibels into the wooded silence. ■

Jim Pearce was a Principal Lecturer in the Faculty of Art & Design at the Harrow College of Higher Education. He runs wildfowl carving courses at the Missenden Abbey Summer School in Buckinghamshire, takes individual students at his workshop in Watford, Herts and is a committee member of the British Decoy & Wildfowl Carvers Association.

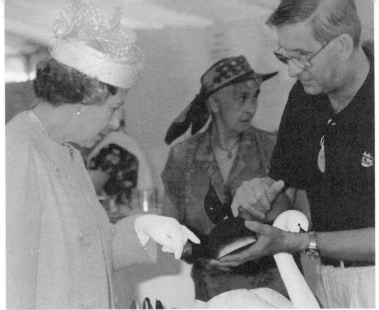

Her Majesty the Queen examining the author's Greenwinged Teal at last year's East of England Show.

ROYAL DUCKS

JAMES C. PEARCE

HOW A MALE AND FEMALE MALLARD WERE CARVED FIT FOR A QUEEN.

The story behind this project begins at Peterborough in July last year at the East of England Show. I had been invited to demonstrate wildfowl woodcarving for three days and on the third day Her Majesty the Queen was due to make a tour of the show. As a consequence, the second day of the show was given over to the security arrangements to ensure the Queen's safety.

In the morning and again in the afternoon my tools, materials and boxes were thoroughly searched by security officers and all the carved ducks, eagles and owls on show were subjected to very close scrutiny. Sniffer dogs also paid me two visits during the day, climbing over everything and frantically searching until they too were satisfied that I was not concealing explosives.

Royal Interest

The Queen had been introduced to the craft of decoy duck carving on a visit she had made to the East coast of America the previous year, and she was clearly delighted and very interested to see that the craft was being practised in this country. She was intrigued by the texturing on the carvings and wanted to know how such realistic feathers could be created in wood. The Queen particularly admired a little female Greenwinged Teal (always a favourite at shows) and a Great Northern Diver (The Loon) which she recognised from her visit to the States. So interested was she, that she stayed to talk for some ten minutes, upsetting a very tight schedule that only allowed for a fleeting visit to the stand.

Preening Green Winged Teal admired by Her Majesty the Queen

Great Northern Diver (Loon) recognised by the Queen from her visits to the USA and Canada

The Follow Up

I knew that whilst she was in the USA she had been presented with a decorative decoy carving by an American artist and so, shortly after I returned from Peterborough, I wrote to her at Buckingham Palace suggesting that she might like an example of the work of an English wildfowl carver. Some days later it was a great pleasure to receive the following reply. 'Her Majesty is delighted to accept the offer and is pleased to leave it to you to decide the exact nature of the carving.' Since the Queen and Prince Philip would certainly have seen Mallards on their Scottish and Norfolk estates I reasoned that the most appropriate choice for the carving would be a male and female Mallard.

The Pattern

Realism is a key feature of decorative decoy carving and the carver must know his subject in every detail. Photographs, paintings and illustrations help in providing the information to ensure accuracy but there is no substitute for observing the subjects themselves in their natural habitat. Armed with this knowledge and a host of references the initial pattern was drawn.

For this I always recommend using a translucent material that is flexible enough to 'mould' round curves on the wood but stiff enough to allow the carver to draw round it onto the wood. No less than three patterns were cut for the Royal Mallards before I was satisfied that I had what I wanted. It is far better to have a wastebin full of unsatisfactory patterns at this stage than a graveyard of carved 'failures' later. The patterns, a side and a top view of the carving, were drawn on the wood and, using a bandsaw, the 'blanks' were cut out.

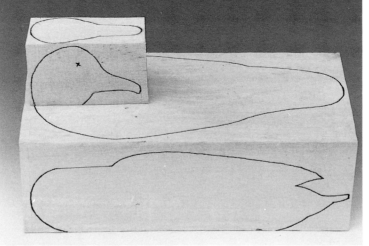

The final pattern for the female Mallard transferred to the wood and ready for the bandsaw

A range of good quality fixed blade knives is a must for the wildfowl carver

---

'It is far better to have a wastebin full of unsatisfactory patterns at the outset than a graveyard of carved "failures" later.'

Carbide cutters used with the Pfingst power tool for speedy 'rough' carving

Carving

The most commonly used wood for wildfowl carving in the UK is jelutong, or 'chewing gum' wood, imported from Malaysia. Defined as a hardwood by virtue of its dense grain, it is nevertheless very light and soft enough to carve easily. It is excellent for texturing as it will hold extremely fine detail and ideal for painting with acrylics or oils.

Preliminary shaping was carried out using a wide variety of tools. I try to get through this stage of 'hogging off' the surplus wood as quickly as possible and so any tool that will remove wood effectively is brought into play. I use knives, carbide, diamond and ruby cutters and a whole range of

power tools, including a recently acquired power chisel which I think is a marvellous weapon and I wonder how I ever managed before without it.

Technology has come to the aid of the impatient woodcarver with the power carver

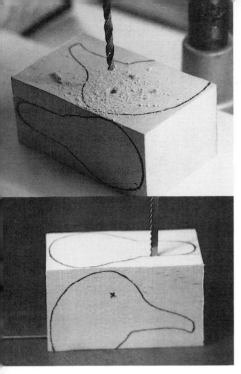

The author putting the finishing touches to the carving

The eye sockets may be drilled before cutting out the rough shape or 'blank' on the bandsaw or later, when carving the head

In wildfowl carving the head is frequently carved separately and attached to the body later

Sanding drums are used to achieve the high degree of smoothness required before texturing

It is quite usual in decoy woodcarving to carve the head separately and, in fact, many carvers prefer the flexibility afforded them by doing so. However, it is not acceptable to merely twist the head into any position when affixing it to the body. With a live bird any movement of the head, such as it makes when preening (the female Mallard in this case), significantly alters the lines of the body and the feather patterns.

Consequently, the final position of the head must be established at the pattern cutting stage. The heads of both ducks were carved separately and attached to the bodies before the sanding operation was started.

Sanding

When the carving process is completed, the entire surface of the wood must be rendered 'baby bottom' smooth. To achieve this I rubbed down initially with a 120 grit sanding material and finished off using 400 or 600 grit. The best sanding material for this job is manufactured in Switzerland and then annoyingly it is exported to the States, from where I buy it at a premium. Even after the most careful of sanding, the surface still requires further treatment before it is ready to accept texturing tools. The apparently smooth surface must be sprayed with de-natured alcohol or water to raise the grain and painstakingly sanded again. Feather texturing on a poorly sanded

surface is difficult and the achievement of **very** fine feathering impossible.

Texturing

Decorative decoy carving is characterised by the realism created by feather texturing. The techniques used are very similar to those employed in pyrography and when first applied in the early days to wildfowl carvings the results were far from encouraging. However, with the development of a wide variety of lighter and sharper burning pens incorporating variable temperature control, the results improved enormously and now the very

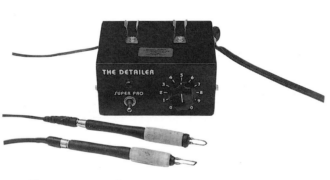

The appearance of soft feathers is created by the careful application of the burning pen to the smooth surface of the wood

Using a variety of small cutters the Electer, NSK, running at speeds up to 30,000 rpm is ideal for creating fine feather texturing

Coarse and fine stones are used with the NSK to form the very 'soft' feathers

finest feather patterns can be simulated in wood.

The equipment used to texture the two Mallards is a Super Pro Detailer, an American burner which requires a step-down transformer to operate at 110 volts. At the time I bought it there was no suitable equivalent piece of equipment on the UK market but now, happily, temperature-controlled pens working on 240 volts are readily available here.

The burning pen is not the only tool used to create feather texturing. On the Mallards, for instance, the larger feathers are profiled, and in some cases undercut, using knives and small rotary cutters. The 'softer' side pocket feathers were relieved using small spherical ruby and diamond cutters while on most of the feather barbs texturing stones were used to augment the effects created by the burning pen. I have found that texturing requires considerable patience and takes an inordinately long time to complete. Nevertheless, it can be regarded by the carver as being therapeutic and very good for soothing the nerves!

Painting

Before any painting is started I always take the completed carving well away from the workshop while it is given a thorough spring clean. Ideally, painting should be undertaken in a room completely separate from the carving area.

To avoid the inconvenience and embarrassment of smudging wet painted areas I always attach a handle to the carvings. In the case of the female Mallard this was

simply a 'keel' fixed to the bottom of the duck with a very small spot of epoxy glue and which was easily removed later with a sharp knock from a hammer. For the male a temporary base was made from waste wood and his feet were firmly clamped to this during the painting operation.

The ducks were treated with two coats of sealant and when this had thoroughly dried, at least three very thin coats of 'gesso' (acrylic primer) were applied; extreme care being taken to avoid clogging up the feathers. Attention to reference sources at this stage is absolutely essential. Having gone to such great lengths to achieve realism in the carving it seems such a pity not to take every precaution to ensure colour fidelity. In this respect, I would warn against using poor colour illustrations as, even in books published to assist bird recognition, poetic licence is all too frequently taken in the matter of colours.

The two ducks were painted in acrylics; Winsor and Newton Acryla range and an American product which I have used for some time now, Jo Sonja paints.

Mounting and Presentation

The carvings were finally mounted on the base three and a half months from the time the first pattern was drawn. A silver hand-engraved inscription was fixed to the base and the presentation was made at Windsor Castle on Her Majesty's birthday 21st April 1992.

Shortly after I received the following letter. ■

The completed carving of the two mallards as presented to HM the Queen

Detail of the head of the male mallard

WINDSOR CASTLE

22nd April, 1992.

Dear Mr Pearce,

It was very good of you and your wife to come to Windsor yesterday with the splendid Mallard carving for The Queen. Her Majesty and The Duke of Edinburgh are delighted with it, and as I predicted to you it looks likely to find a home at Sandringham. It has been much admired by all The Queen's guests. Her Majesty has asked me to send you her very warm thanks for this most welcome birthday present, and her good wishes.

Yours sincerely,

Kenneth Scott.

(KENNETH SCOTT)

J. C. Pearce, Esq.

David Stokes started to write during long periods of illness that started in 1988. Up until then he had spent most of his working life in the tele-communications and computer industries servicing and installing hardware.

To back up his articles with pictures he took up photography attending courses at Maidstone Adult Education Centre.

In 1990 his job became redundant and with help from the Enterprise Allowance Scheme he made his hobby his business.

A rocking horse
see-saw

BACKING THE
RIGHT
HORSE
DAVID STOKES

A successful rocking horse factory where most of the carving is still done by hand.

The rocking horse is alive and well and still being made in Bethersden in the English county of Kent. This is a unique factory, this year celebrating its first ten years of producing rocking horses of the highest possible quality; it is run by twins Marc and Tony Stevenson.

I met Marc at the company's workshop where he explained the history and the methods of making these magnificent Victorian-style nursery toys: 'Our uncle made rocking horses for 40 years, as children my brother and I remember seeing them,' Marc told me.

'Ten years ago we looked around and found that no-one was making a traditional rocking horse. This inspired us to ask him to teach us how to make them. Initially he didn't think it was a good idea, when we put

a thousand pounds in front of him he saw that we meant business and he gave Tony an apprenticeship. We took it from there.

'One thing we did was to decide to number each horse. Starting from 001, we have now reached our first thousand. Number 1000 will be a very special horse indeed, probably made from rosewood, we haven't decided what to do with it yet, but it will be a very special horse.'

I asked how the recession was affecting business, Marc was very confident: 'We had our best year in 1991. When everyone else is feeling the recession, rocking horses have done very well. Every year up to 1991 we have upped our production and I don't see why that growth curve shouldn't continue. We are routinely evolving products and aiming at the best quality possible. We do not go after quantity, a horse will take as long as it takes, each normally taking around five to seven weeks depending what sort it is. So it's about three a week. We can produce more than that when the need arises.

'We use a variety of timbers. We started off just making dapple grey rocking horses because they are traditional. For those we use tulip wood for the body, and beech for the legs and the stands of those on the Victorian safety stand. Horses on the Georgian bow have the same timber in the horse, but elm or oak for the bow. We have had to start using oak for the bow because of the demise of the elm in Britain.

'After the great hurricane of 1987 many specimen trees were lost, the authorities cleared away the timber in indecent haste. If they had only thought timber, not debris, we would have a wonderful reserve of hitherto rare woods. Some estate owners, whose trees were felled by the wind, came to us to turn the tree into "something nice"; obviously, as they were talking to us, that meant a horse.'

The company also makes tricycles, with metal wheels built around a horse. They took the idea from old drawings and were commissioned by some European doll makers. Also in the catalogue is a pull along toy, a little cart with a horse on wheels.

More wooden toys are planned using much of the left over wood, off-cuts and the like. It's all too good to throw away and there is room in the toy market for good old-fashioned toys, to go alongside the electronic computerised toys that everyone thought would oust the more traditional toys.

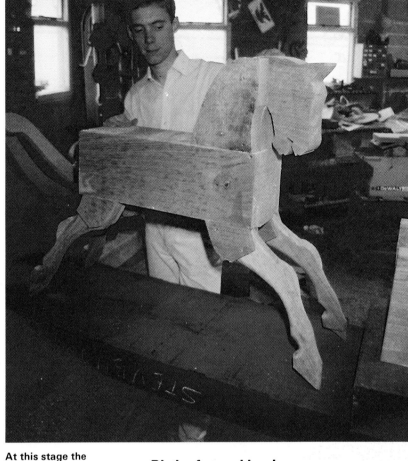

At this stage the horse is very square but recognisably a horse

The body box, glued and clamped

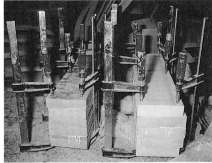

To make the legs and head David uses a band saw

The body box complete and ready for gluing

Birth of a rocking horse

Marc took me around the workshop to see just how these world famous horses are constructed. All around the workshop are examples of the new mixing with the old, modern power tools, and traditional hand tools that would be recognised by carpenters hundreds of years ago.

Modern production methods have not found favour in Bethersden. I thought I would follow the route an embryo horse would take through the workshop. They start as unprepossessing blocks of wood, these are glued and clamped together to make a very thick-walled closed box. This is the main body of the horse.

David's job is blocking-up the horse from pieces of wood. He also makes the stands, Victorian or Georgian. Horses are made up of 25 different pieces of wood, legs, head, neck, muscle blocks and the seven pieces that go into making up the body.

While the glue is setting David marks out the legs, head and neck on to the chosen woods using templates, afterwards cutting them out on an enormous bandsaw. The head and neck are mortised and tennoned and glued into place. The Stevensons are proud of the fact that no metal fixings are used, except in fastening on the Georgian bows and in the assembly of the Victorian stand.

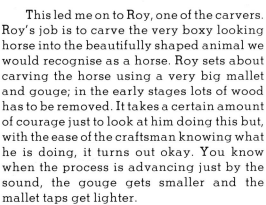

John carves the boxey horse. 'You know when the process is advancing just by the sound, the gouge gets smaller and the mallet taps get lighter'

David Bates sands the horse down when John has finished with mallet and gouge

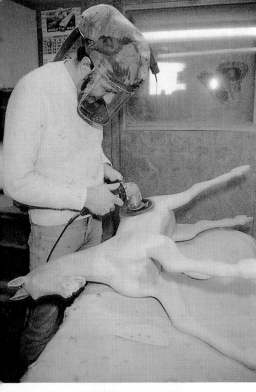

This led me on to Roy, one of the carvers. Roy's job is to carve the very boxy looking horse into the beautifully shaped animal we would recognise as a horse. Roy sets about carving the horse using a very big mallet and gouge; in the early stages lots of wood has to be removed. It takes a certain amount of courage just to look at him doing this but, with the ease of the craftsman knowing what he is doing, it turns out okay. You know when the process is advancing just by the sound, the gouge gets smaller and the mallet taps get lighter.

When the carving is finished the horse has to be smoothed and made ready for painting or varnishing. David Bates is the expert sander. Using progressively finer abrasive papers the horse becomes smoother and, after hours of hand sanding, is ready for the tender care of the finishing department.

Upstairs I found Neil Wilcox, a young man whose job it is to make all the tack. Bridles and saddles come into shape under his skilled hands. 'They are hand made from carefully selected leather. Everything is made on site except the stirrups and the glass eyes, those we buy in.

'The other part of my job is to provide each horse with a mane and tail, these are genuine horse hair. The hair comes in big hanks from all over the world.'

In the next room was Michelle Coverley; her task is to stain and beeswax the horses, bringing them to a very high gloss. 'I work as assistant to the finisher. We put on two

Neil Wilcox shows off the hanks of real horse hair

Michelle puts the final finish to a Victorian stand

A horse's head, with glass eye inserted, is ready for finishing

The beautifully finished head

coats of stain and then apply a special varnish, then we put on beeswax until we get the finish you see now. Lovely, isn't it?'

In another part of the workshop is the restoration department run by John, the company's 'horse doctor'. Like the rest of Stevenson's staff he is enthusiastic about his job.

Rocking horses at home and at play on Victorian safety stands

'We at Stevenson's,' he says, 'have a good understanding of how wood behaves, our horses are as good as any that have ever been made. Some of the horses that come in for restoration were made over 100 years ago, in the days that everybody says, "they don't make them like that any more"; good job too! I've found splitting wood held together with nails and the splits filled with plaster. The way older horses were constructed, the more they were used, the looser they became. Ours are made in such a way, if anything, they tighten up when used.' ∎

Les Jewell served an apprentice-ship with an internationally well-known ecclesiastical firm in Exeter, Devon.

With the exception of the war years, when he served with the Royal Engineers in North Africa and in Italy, he has been constantly employed as a carver and sculptor. He has work in very many churches in the UK and abroad, notably in America, in Washington DC and Cleveland, Ohio. In 1984 he gained the *Craftsman of the Year Award* for his part in the restoration of St. John's Cathedral in Jacksonville, Florida. He is a member of the Master Carvers, the oldest body of professional carvers and sculptors in Great Britain.

Les has also had success with his wild-life sculpture, gaining awards in different years at the Royal West of England Academy. He is a teacher with the Devon Education Authority, taking carving classes mostly with adults. He also lectures to a wide selection of audiences and is a member of the British Woodcarvers Association.

THE BITER BIT

LES JEWELL

A MASTER CARVER DESCRIBES HOW HE PLANNED AND MADE THIS AWARD-WINNING SCULPTURE GROUP WITH A STORY.

In any sculpture group I do, I try if possible to tell a story. In this one, which I have named *The Biter Bit,* I have used a buzzard, weasels and harvest mice. In chasing the mice the weasels have been surprised by the bird which has caught one of them.

If there is a moral to this it is: if you have your eye on something, just look out someone isn't watching *you*!

Within quite a short distance from where I live in Devon there is countryside and woods holding all the wild animal life normal to this area, living in their natural state. It was while I was watching a buzzard hunting that the idea came to me, and from then on I was impatient to start.

I visited a small saw-mill, the owner of which I know well. On telling him of my intention he considered for a moment and then said, "I've got the very thing for you" — and so it proved. It was an oak butt which he knew had been lying in a corner for many years.

With his tractor he dragged it over to the saw-pit, and with the first cut I knew it was what I was looking for — mellow and by the smell of it, dry. I decided to take it.

As the figures were going to be life-sized, I was going to need a big piece of wood. The main portion I chose was 54″ 1370mm long x 15″ 380mm square and was so heavy it took three people to get it up on to the bench in my workshop. And this was only the body of the bird and all the other animals.

The bird's wings were added on afterwards. Apart from the fact that it would have taken an enormous amount of wood to do it in one piece, it was not practical. By joining the wings it was possible to get them the long and strong way of the grain (FIG 1). When these were fitted much later, the whole piece was about 36″ 915mm high.

When tackling a big lump of wood, and not being sure if it is completely dry, I try to get as much of the dross off as soon as possible. This helps to minimise the cracking that will take place if it has still some wetness in it.

I got the whole thing roughed out down to ½″ 12mm of the final finish. Because it was not possible to kiln dry a piece as big as this I had to watch it very closely. I

Detail of the bird's
head and captured
weasel.

He took the two pieces of oak for the wings, each 36" 915mm x 20" 510mm x 3½" 90mm which I provided and he first formed a tenon on each (FIG 1). Then with me holding them at the right slant he marked the mortises. These he cut at the correct angle from the pitch I had made and which we could sight through.

Using the drawbore method he then drilled the holes. The advantage of using this method is that a drawbore pin — a piece of steel, a sort of enlarged skewer — can be used for holding the wings to the body when getting the fit right (FIG 2).

When I was satisfied with the marking out of the shape of the wings I knocked out the pins and completed the carving of them flat on the bench, every now and again trying them on again, leaving just a bit of odding by the joint.

Anyone who carves finds he is at a disadvantage. A painter can make an eagle fly free, soaring in the sky on canvas, but sculpture is eternally chained to the ground. I usually have more trouble forming a base than I do in the execution, and so it proved in this case.

For obvious reasons I could not leave the buzzard with just its legs in contact with the base. If I wanted it to remain intact I had to strengthen it, and so I had to design a support for the tail.

I took a part of a blackberry shrub for this, and as I couldn't just have a little piece at the back I had to trail it along the whole length. It worked out well in the end, but it was an extra I hadn't reckoned on in the first place.

When I had finished all the carving I finally fixed the wings by gluing them and driving home a glued oak pin. The pin when faired off was invisible, as I was able to lose it in the contours of one of the feathers. I then cleaned off the odding on the wing joints.

Finally I sealed the work with a matt varnish and polished it with natural beeswax which I had mixed with white spirit.

I exhibited it at quite a few prestigious exhibitions, including the Royal West of England Academy where in 1988 it won the award of the best piece voted by the general public. It has since been sold to a private collector.■

knew that if any shakes, or splits, were to happen it would be in the thickest part, which happened to be the body of the bird, and just in case the worst happened I kept some of the wood which I had cut off the back of it.

These I kept for shivers, wedge-shaped pieces used to fill cracks. As these came from the area

Roughed out carving showing the mortise for the wings.

FIG 1 Detail of the wing shape.

FIG 2 Drawbore pin fixing for holding on the wings.

where I expected trouble, there would be nothing to show if shivers were used. In the event I had to use only one.

If oak is wet your tools go black after using them. In my experience this only applies to oak, and as mine were still shining it was obvious the sawyer was as good as his word!

Having already painted the ends to stop air cracks, I then covered it over with a cloth and left it in a dark corner of my workshop. There it stayed while I got on with other work.

From time to time I inspected it, tapping in the shiver as the crack got wider, until one day I saw it being forced out as the opening began closing up again. When I was satisfied it was right I put glue on it and tapped it home. When I finally cleaned it off, the line was invisible. The whole waiting period took six months.

The drawbore pin

Now it was time to start again, and the first thing to do was to join the wings to the body. A precise job like this was out of my range, so I went to Dave the skilled joiner who works with me.

If you have never carved wood before, a stylised hedgehog is a good introduction. In carving it, you will learn how to make a rounded shape, some detailing of features, some texturing and finishing methods – skills that will be used for further work.

Almost any wood will do, as long as it is sound and straight grained. Avoid woods with the stripy appearance of interlocking grain, as this will cause problems. You could use a half-round log or, as I did for this project, a block. It was a mahogany block about 7 x 4 x 3in, 180 x 100 x 75mm, with the grain along its length. You will make faster progress with a softer wood.

Drawing

First step is to make some sketches. Their purpose is not to produce an artistic creation, but to make you think three-dimensionally. Think what shape your carving is to be from all aspects – top, both sides, front and back. The best way to have a clear idea in your mind is to draw it: this forces you to think.

All you need is the outline of each aspect, to show the wood to be removed first.

Draw the outlines on the wood. Fill the area as far as possible (you will have less wood to remove) but it must be well proportioned and not too long for its height. Draw in a centre line, running from nose to rear end. Keep your sketches to hand for easy reference.

Back end

The bottom of the block should be level and smooth, a job best done with a plane or Surform.

Mark the point on the back end which will be the apex of the rear curve. Start with a ⅝in, 15mm or ½in, 13mm No9 gouge. Place the cutting edge about ¾in, 20mm from the back end of the block, on one of the top corners. You will be cutting outwards, and with the grain.

Give the gouge a sharp tap with the mallet – not too heavily or the corners of the tool will go

PRICKLY PERSONALITY

A SIMPLE HEDGEHOG IS AN EASY INTRODUCTION TO THE SKILLS OF WOODCARVING, AS ZOË GERTNER SHOWS

beneath the surface of the wood. Drop your gouge hand slightly then steadily tap with the mallet, continuing almost until the edge of the wood. Do not shoot off the end but gradually raise your gouge hand while approaching the edge. Guide the cut over and round the corner of the block, aiming towards the apex mark.

Begin the second cut a little further forward in the same 'furrow', finishing nearer the apex than before. Remember to lift your hand each time you approach the edge of the block. Work rows of cuts, either side of this first furrow. Remove an equal amount of wood from each side, aiming for the apex with each stroke. Go on to

Shaping the rear, the cuts aimed towards the apex mark

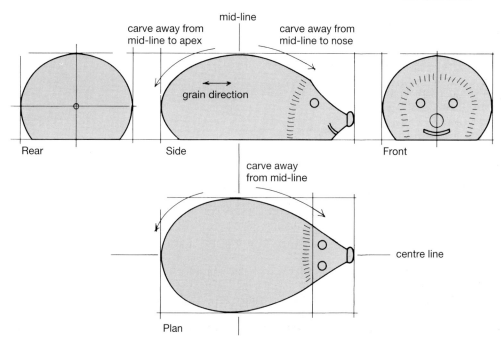

carve away from mid-line to apex

carve away from mid-line to nose

mid-line

grain direction

Rear

Side

Front

carve away from mid-line

centre line

Plan

the other corners, working in the same way.

Start the next set of cuts closer to the rear edge of the wood. Cut deeper and steeper, heading towards the apex mark with a short steep cut, taking off the back corner. Each successive set of cuts should become longer until you have cut the whole end surface, up to the apex.

Halfway point

Draw a line around the middle of the hedgehog – you will need to round off the upper corners as far back as this line. Slightly twist the gouge as you cut round, so it cuts over the corners and towards the apex.

The rounded end should be symmetrical, so redraw the centre line from nose to tail and compare the shapes on either side of it to see what needs removing. Mark the waste wood, and remove it little by little. Check frequently, do not spend too much time on one area and work towards the apex across the end, until the shape is symmetrical. It is important to get a good shape at this stage, or your hedgehog will not look right in the end.

You will notice that it is harder cutting across end-grain, as you progress towards the apex. It is particularly important that your gouges are sharp when carving a softer wood. Dull tools will tear out fibres rather than slicing them cleanly. If you find little tufts adhering to the cutting edge, or a score mark in the same place within each cut, stop carving and sharpen the gouge – it is blunt.

The head

Mark the middle of the nose, low down on the centre line. The face is cone-like, and shaping starts in the same way as for the rear end. However, when approaching the front edge of the wood don't lift your gouge hand. Keep each cut directed straight towards the nose.

Work round all four sides, making longer runs from the upper corners and shorter ones along the base. Leave a small flat area, about ¼in, 6mm across on the tip, so the hedgehog can be held lengthways

in the vice.

Work round from the sides to bring the snout tidily into the body. If the snout is too short, take away more wood from the upper corners, so the face starts from further back along the body. If the snout becomes too wide, remove equal amounts of wood from both sides.

Round the front of the body back to the mid-line then turn the hedgehog round and blend the front and rear curves together.

Smoothing

Ridges left by the No9 gouge need to be removed. This is done using a Surform, rasp, or a large No3 (No2 Swiss) gouge. Once the ridges have been reduced, turn the gouge bevel uppermost and, still using the mallet, carefully slice towards the centre line. Guide the tool around the shape with shallow cuts, ensuring that the corners of the gouge don't score the surface as you work. Should this happen, pare away the scratch and the area surrounding it. Redraw the centre line every time it is removed.

Surform or rasp marks and scratches must be removed using the No3 gouge, or use a convex soled spokeshave.

With the centre line as reference, look at the shape of the wood and feel with your hands for lumps or flatnesses. Mark these then remove them with shallow paring cuts. Repeat the whole process until you are satisfied that the hedgehog is comfortably rounded. Sometimes it helps to close your eyes when feeling for irregularities.

TOOL LIST

¼in, 6mm skew chisel
¼in, 6mm No3 gouge
1in, 25mm No3 gouge
½in, 13mm No9 gouge
⅛in, 3mm v-tool
Mallet
Garnet paper 120-320 grit
Wax polishes
(Surform or rasp, convex soled spokeshave optional)

As shaping continues, a combination of straight and spiralling cuts is used

Shaping the front, straight cuts on the snout are blended into the convex curve of the body

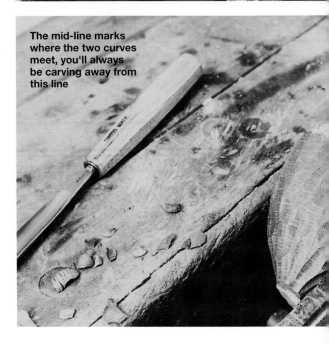

The mid-line marks where the two curves meet, you'll always be carving away from this line

Scraping

In all carving it is essential to have a good clean surface on which to put detail or texturing. This is prepared using a scraper to remove irregularities and marks remaining from the previous tools. Start close to the nose, working round scraping towards the tip. Work back until you reach the mid-line, then scrape the rear end. Begin at the apex mark, and scrape towards it from all round. Take extra care at the mid-line not to scrape against the grain. If the surface becomes woolly or dull you have gone too far over the mid-line.

Feel the surface to make sure you don't miss scraping any part, and don't forget underneath. At the end of each scraping stroke, lift the scraper off the surface – don't drag it back against the wood fibres.

eyes, on the end-grain of a scrap piece of the same wood you are using. Start with a large circle, and make a clean cut right round to join up neatly, at the same depth where you started. Go on to practise circles the same size as the eyes on the hedgehog. Try to complete each circle in one continuous sweep, moving yourself round as you cut. When you are confident, go on to your hedgehog.

Pare away the outer edge of the v-cut, cutting with the grain, leaving the eye proud of the surface. Use the corner of a ¼in, 6mm No3 gouge. Push with the right hand, and control the forward movement with the left finger and thumb. Be careful not to catch the corner of the gouge in the eye.

Remove pencil marks and gouge marks around the eye by scraping with a No3 gouge. Be sure to scrape with the grain.

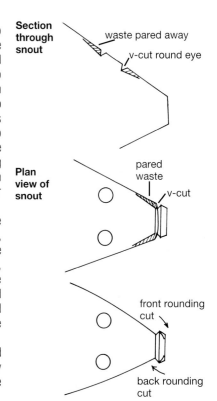

Section through snout — waste pared away — v-cut round eye

Plan view of snout — pared waste — v-cut

front rounding cut

back rounding cut

Face details

Mark the junction between body and face, draw on eyes, nose and mouth, making sure they are placed symmetrically. The nose is carved last, as it is most vulnerable.

Using a small v-tool (⅛in, 3mm or ³⁄₁₆in, 5mm) practise cutting

Two simple hedgehogs, the right from a half log of elm, the left from a block of mahogany

Paring into the v-groove around the eye, across the end-grain and down the snout

Zoë Gertner is a professional woodcarver and teacher. She has taught people aged from 8 to 85 years old. Commissioned works have included a proscenium for a fairground organ and pew ends in Wedmore church, Somerset. Her work can be found in collections all over the world.

Near the mid-line chips from the prickles need to be nipped out with a skew chisel

Paring round the feet into the v-cut to leave them proud of the underside

The mouth

Cut the line of the mouth with the v-tool in one continuous cut. Round the sharp edges of the v-cut using the ¼in, 6mm No3 gouge, paring towards the centre line. Then scrape the pared surfaces gently with the gouge edge.

Prickles

Draw the general lines of the prickles, starting with a fringe around the face, continuing along the body, to converge at the apex at the rear end. The prickles are short even cuts with a v-tool, which must not run into each other. They should be staggered, row by row, and flow tidily along the body.

Start about ⅜in, 10mm back from the fringe line and cut towards the line – each cut finishing on the line. Start at the top, work round one side of the face, then round the other. Use the mallet with the v-tool, cut in for about five taps, then drop the gouge hand to lift out the chip cleanly.

Position the second row of prickles between the first, so that they don't run into each other. Work back, row by row. The chips will not come out cleanly when you are cutting along the grain on top of the body. Don't pull the chip, but nip it off using the point of a ¼in, 6mm skew chisel.

When you reach the mid-line, stop, turn the hedgehog round and begin texturing the rear. Start at

the apex with short cuts that converge on the mark. Work forwards and gradually cover the rear end until you reach the mid-line. Check that the whole body has been textured, and there are no bald patches.

The feet

Draw the outlines of pads and claws on the underside of the hedgehog. Cut round the outlines with the v-tool, in one continuous sweep if possible. Using the corner of the ¼in, 6mm No3 gouge, pare away the outer area of each v-cut so the pads and claws stand proud. Scrape the pared surface smooth.

The nose

Draw a ring just behind the flat end of the snout and cut along it with the v-tool. This forms a channel into which the nose can be shaped to make it button-like.

Shave away the snout to meet the v-channel, using a ¼in, 6mm No3 gouge. Control these cuts carefully. Do not overshoot into the nose itself. Do not lever the gouge at the end of each cut or you could lift the nose off. Withdraw the tool in the same plane as the cut and the nose will be quite safe.

If the nose tip is too large, undercut it, with the flute of the gouge against the nose tip. This cut should be at a steep angle across the grain, not directly into it or it may split. Cut all round the

nose tip, then make meeting cuts from the snout side. Repeat these cuts to reduce the tip to the appropriate size. Pare away the snout to blend it into the rest of the face.

To round off the end of the nose, carefully pare the outer edge over, working towards the centre with a slicing cut. Use the ¼in, 6mm No3 gouge, bevel uppermost. Continue until no flatness remains on the tip. Scrape it smooth, working towards the centre.

Finishing

Check over the carving for rough areas, sharp edges or odd whiskers not cleanly cut. Use the point of the skew chisel to clean up – it can also be used to scrape.

Rub down the carving with garnet paper, 120 or 220 grit. But not too vigorously, or the carefully carved features become indistinct.

Be prepared to spend a lot of time on the finish – finishing should be done meticulously, or your carving will lack quality.

Apply a coat of cheap colourless wax polish to show up blemishes. Use an old toothbrush to apply the wax and brush it well into the texturing. Imperfections exposed must be pared away, the surrounding area scraped and then re-textured. Re-coat with polish and check again.

While the carving is damp with polish, rub it with 220 or 320 grit garnet paper. The dust will mix with the polish, giving a very smooth surface. Brush the excess out of the prickle furrows, and feel over the hedgehog for remaining imperfections.

Finally, apply a good quality colourless wax polish, leave overnight, then buff up with a lint-free duster. Repeat this several times and handle the carving as much as you can to build up the patina.

Staining is not advised as the stain is absorbed more in the end-grain, giving an uneven result.

You have now completed your hedgehog. If it is your first piece, it is something to be proud of. Show it off as much as possible. I hope you will be inspired to continue carving. ∎

CAROUSEL CHARGER

ANTHONY DEW

A COLOURFUL HORSE WITH CARVED MANE AND HARNESS.

Starting to rough carve ears and nostrils

I have long admired beautifully carved horses on fairground carousels, and felt that I would like to have a go at making one, or something like one. The opportunity arose when I was planning my new book *The Rocking Horse Maker*.

I had already developed a number of rocking-horse designs to suit most woodworking and carving abilities — from a simple little horse for toddlers to the fully carved Victorian style of rocking horse in various sizes — but needed a project that would present something of a challenge to the more ambitious woodcarver. With all its saddlery, bridle and mane carved into the wood, rather than being made of leather and hair as is the case with the traditional rocking horse, a carousel-style horse seemed to be just the thing.

We have in our collection of rocking horses a couple of small English carousel horses dating from the early part of this century. They are not as fancy as some larger horses, which can be extremely elaborate and flamboyantly carved, but they do have most of the features characteristic of the traditional carousel horse, and the construction seemed fairly straightforward. It was along the lines of these that I decided to base my version of the design.

The head (including the ears) and central part of the neck could be cut from a single piece of 3in, 75mm thick timber. I used kiln dried tulipwood (American poplar) which I find to be an excellent carving timber and, at the present time anyway, readily available in a wide variety of thicknesses and

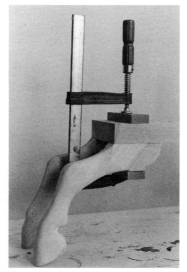

Cramping legs to the lower body block

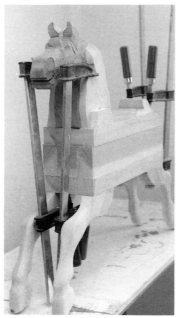

Final cramping of body and neck muscle blocks

widths. Lime, sycamore, or even basswood would also be good for this project.

The horse is made up from sixteen blocks of timber, glued together with Cascamite, a resin based adhesive. The legs are mortised into the body, but all the other pieces are simply butt jointed together, reinforced with fluted dowel pegs. The body is a hollow rectangular box made up from 2in, 50mm thick timber and, although a lot is removed in the carving process, there is virtually no chance of carving through to the hollow in the middle (which would obviously be a disaster). Although I did a little preliminary shaping of the head and lower legs prior to blocking up, the carving really starts when the whole horse has been assembled.

Showing rough carved bridle

Hollowing the ears — glass eyes have been set in filler

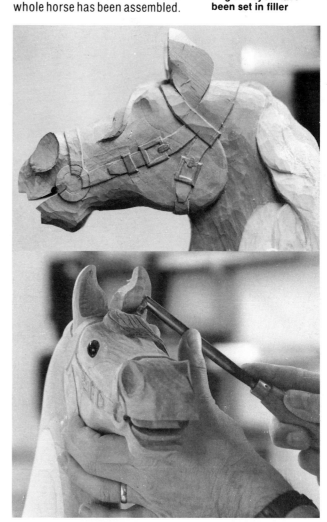

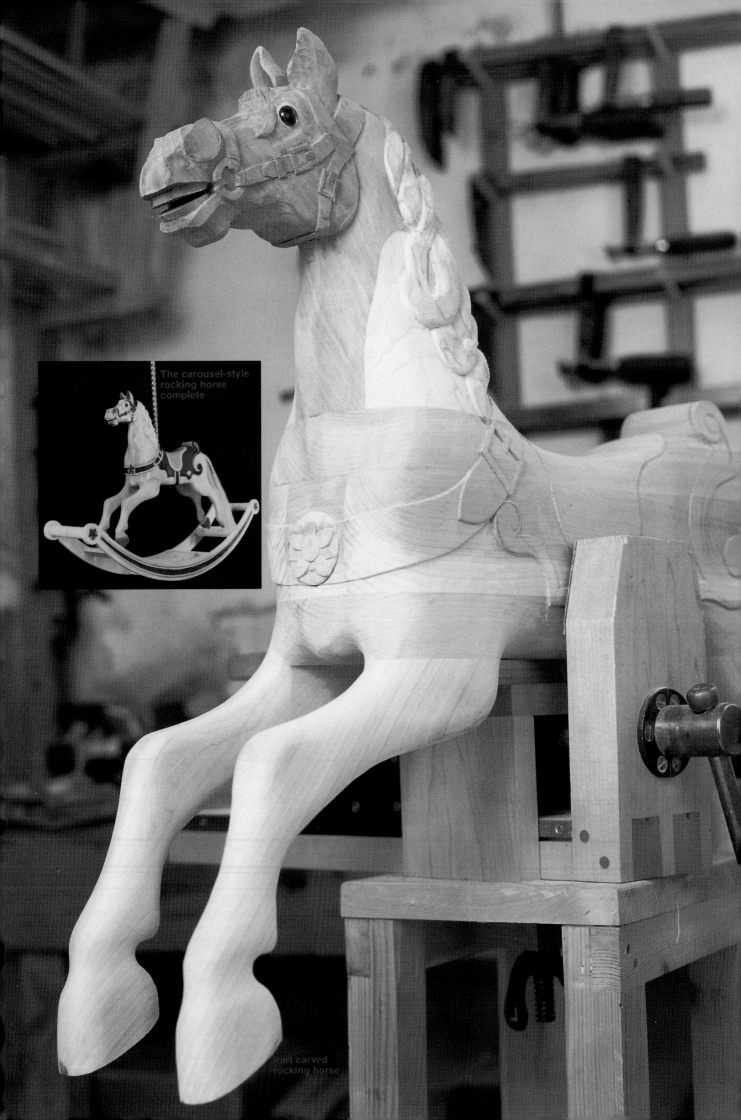

The carousel-style rocking horse complete

Part carved rocking horse

Using v-tool on back of saddle

Detail of the chest rosette

Carving details of the saddlery

Carousel-style

The main difficulty in carving a carousel style horse, especially for a rocking horse maker like me, is to make due allowance for the thickness of all the saddlery, bridle, mane and forelock hair. You have to be careful that you do not go and carve off some piece which you subsequently realise should not have been removed. It is unsatisfactory, and hurts the pride, to have to glue back bits inadvertently carved away. By the time the carving is completed all squareness should have gone, and the tack should look as if it is buckled onto the horse, not incised into it.

As with most carving projects, it is preferable to rough carve the whole thing without worrying too much about the detail, rather than attempt to carve one small area to completion and then move on.

Starting with the head, the shapes of the ears are pencilled in and separated with a coping saw. The full width of the timber is needed at the ears and eyebrows, but the head tapers down towards the mouth which finishes just under 2in, 50mm wide. I kept pencilling in the position of the bridle straps so as not to forget where they should be, and used a straight chisel to cut along the edges of the straps before paring away on the waste side of the line with a shallow sweep No. 4 gouge. The rough carving of the body and neck was done with a 1¼in, 32mm No. 8 alongee gouge and mallet.

Once a reasonably satisfactory overall shape has been achieved, the top and flaps of the saddle and straps can be rough sanded in order to easily pencil in the exact positions of the saddlery and straps. 'Stitch' lines on the saddlery can be cut with a v-tool, which can also be used to mark the flow of the hair. I am not very practised at carving hair and consequently not very good at it, but I tried to achieve a pleasing flow of forelock and mane hair, interweaving it a little. The mane was up to ¾in, 19mm proud of the neck in places, while the bridle, martingale and girth straps were made to stand about ⅛in-³/₁₆in, 3-5mm proud of the horse — more in places where two or more straps had to cross.

It is important to keep carving gouges sharp — I use a steel cutting compound on a 6in, 150mm calico mop mounted in a small bench grinder for honing — particularly for the hair, which then needs very little sanding

Detail of a hoof

down. In any case sanding should be done carefully to avoid losing the sharpness of the carving. Glass eyes are held in recesses with woodfiller and the ears and nostrils are hollowed out. Some muscling on the neck will enhance the appearance, as will some details such as horseshoes and shoe nails, buckle holes and teeth.

Painted pony

Traditionally, of course, carousel horses are decorated with many bright colours, and I opted for a painted finish reminiscent of this tradition, although not without a slight pang of regret at the thought of covering all that careful carving with paint. Acrylic paints are easy to use and quick-drying, as well as being readily available in small tubes, in many bright and interesting colours. Acrylic paints do need to be varnished over with a clear satin varnish or they will fingermark all too easily. The impression of a carousel horse is enhanced by the spiral brass pole. This fits over a length of dowel which inserts into a hole drilled through the body towards the front of the saddle.

Then there are the rockers. These are made up to two parallel arcs of plywood, connected together with cross pieces and with a thin plywood platform in the middle. The horse stands on two of the crosspieces, secured with a single woodscrew up into each hoof, and the two end cross pieces are turned with decorative beads. The rocker arrangement is also given a painted and varnished finish.

When it was finished I felt this little horse looked and worked well — not only a fascinating project to make, but a delightful carousel horse that could be used as a plaything, or simply grace any room as a decorative artifact. ∎

Photographs reproduced with the author's permission from *The Rocking Horse Maker* by Anthony Dew, published by David & Charles. Full size plans for the carousel-style rocking horse are available at a price of £11.99, including VAT and postage, from: The Rocking Horse Shop, Fangfoss, York, YO4 5QH, England. Tel: 01759 368 737. Fax: 01759 368 194.

INTEGRITY IN WOOD

SUSAN HALL

Grainger McKoy one of the foremost bird carvers in the United States talks about his work.

Black skimmer, 1983, basswood, walnut, metal and glass, 24½in 620mm high

Susan Hall is a freelance writer on art subjects.

She gained a bachelor's degree in art history from Moore College of Art and Design in Philadelphia.

Susan is also a photographer. She lives in Philadelphia.

Photographs by Ted Borg

When he was a boy, Grainger McKoy's grandmother gave him a wooden decoy duck for Christmas. He says that the decoy triggered something in him. McKoy compares this to being on the starting blocks at the beginning of a race. McKoy recognises the gift he was given and has developed a deep appreciation for how, as he states, 'We are suspended in all this beauty . . . observing beauty and where it all comes from.' His awareness of the gift makes him handle it more 'gently'. Instrumental in the way he deals with his gift has been his religious conversion, the result of an experience with a dying school friend.

After his religious discovery, he began to look at life differently. McKoy says: 'I am constantly seeking the truth in the material and the subject matter. I am reproducing and trying to represent from whence it came. That includes being sensitive to handling it all correctly from the shipping, to making sure that the person who commissioned the work is given a fair bill of goods . . . I use the word integrity, trying to maintain it, in the whole sphere of my work . . . being obedient to the gift given and recognising it as a gift . . not representing something incorrectly.'

Much of McKoy's work represents the fragility of life and his true religious commitment: 'I can produce something and put it behind plexiglass . . . and protect it but, essentially, everything in the room of the exhibition, 'Bird Sculpture in Wood', at the Brandywine River Museum has a certain life expectancy; even the pyramids have fallen down.

'And when everything is boiled away, someday, everything I produce will be dust. Nothing is forever, except real art that is occurring in my heart. Really, the work I produce in my hands, in my profession, is a playing field for me to have a deeper relationship with my God.'

His work changed after his spiritual transformation, from aggressive carvings, like *Red-shouldered Hawks* and *Copperhead Snake*, 1974 to the contemplative *Dead Plover*, 1980.

Apprenticeship

McKoy's allegiance to art was nurtured under the guidance of a renowned sculptor and naturalist, Gilbert Maggioni of Beaufort, South Carolina. Maggioni spotted McKoy's talent in his youth and invited him to be his apprentice. McKoy changed his course from architecture to zoology at Clemson University, from where he graduated with a degree. Master and student worked together for eighteen months. McKoy says that his mentor discovered a certain gift, because he had the gift also. He credits Maggioni with encouraging him at a unique time in his life. Maggioni was a keen observer of nature and he helped McKoy to see.

Together, they perfected the skill of inserting individually carved feathers into the bird: 'Gilbert was one of the forerunners of that, and I fell on the heels of his experimenting. I was in the right place at the right time.'

One of the most valuable tools Maggioni taught McKoy was his seasoned advice, 'Cultivate what's in your soil, and don't cultivate what other people think should be in your soil.' Together, the pair travelled and studied great art works. McKoy says of Maggioni: 'He influenced me

Carolina parakeets, 1992, basswood, metal and glass, 88in 2235mm high

Least bittern, 1987, basswood, walnut, metal and glass, 30in 760mm high

Dead plover, 1980, unpainted basswood

always to look at my work as an art form and not as a craft or woodcarving, but as sculpture, as fine art.'

McKoy, feels that wood is not viewed as classical artistic material, the art world does not consider it permanent. Grinling Gibbons, the 17th century English sculptor, had an affect on him, because of his handling of wood. 'He took it to such a unique and elevated level,' says McKoy.

Gibbons was appointed by the Crown as Repairer of Carved Wood and Master Sculptor and Carver in Wood. He was known for his naturalism and his work with Christopher Wren. McKoy says that Gibbons really treated woodcarving as an art form. His compositions are beautiful.

Wood sculpture

McKoy believes that wood is not appreciated for its artistic qualities: If you go to any museum or art school, it is thought of as building material. Things permanent are usually associated with granite, stone, casting material and bronze, things you would see outside Windsor Castle.

'You think of Michelangelo as one of the great sculptors but, you don't think of wood. Wood needs to be protected. It is not a stable material because it cracks, it doesn't weather or last under extreme conditions like other materials and so it has been used for interior building and decorating. Wood is what you put around pictures, in frames and for coffins . . . it's short term.'

He has the utmost respect for wood, 'Wood is the medium I choose to work with, whatever comes out of that is out of my hands.' Other great artists have inspired him such as the 19th century American painter, Winslow Homer, American artists Andrew Wyeth and the Brandywine School.

McKoy's compositions are known for their precise detail and 'trompe l'oeil' effect. He refers to himself as a realist, 'I won't

compromise in portraying the bird properly.' He says that he is '. . . honouring a gift. Honour the bird. Honour the subject that's what I do, how I do it, where I do it. If I am sculpting a bird that has a certain number of feathers on one wing, I honour that. I can't give it more or less than that, unless I show a spot missing.' He advises artists to get to know their subject so they will not misrepresent it.

McKoy doesn't alter the subject: 'I won't distort dimensions. I try not to distort so I won't lose the integrity of the bird. There are some distortions in my work if it's done to express the bird in a way that nobody has seen before.

'It is one thing for you to say "I can't believe it's wood" which is a positive statement and I welcome that, but part of me wants to say "but won't you believe it's wood?" Let's appreciate wood. Not only is it a bird, but, it's a bird in wood; let's rejoice! It's another thing trying to fool someone and become too successful,' says McKoy. *Wood Duck in a Croker Sack*, made in 1993, risks the distortion about which he philosophises.

McKoy speaks of a personal integrity when approaching an art work: 'I appreciate detail and I appreciate realism, but I also appreciate wood.' *Black Skimmer*, 1983 and *Green winged Teal*, 1981 support this statement.

Paint or not

The artist is presently working on two life size brown pelicans in flight. He says: 'The pelicans, in walnut, are being left unpainted because I want to show the wood. The walnut is known for its beauty and grain so I'm not going to add any pigment.'

He often works in basswood and, more recently, in a wood indigenous to the area, tupelo. He '. . . chooses birds and subject matter that give something to work with. If I were carving birds in tupelo or basswood, they would not be as attractive left in the raw, unpainted. The end result determines the kind of wood I'll use. Tupelo and basswood are lighter woods that require less structure.' McKoy uses elaborate metal armatures.

The surfaces of his wood carvings are painted with oil paint or left unpainted. The feathers are realistically carved so that one has the instinct to touch the texture of the feathers and the background. The carvings are deftly executed and easily deceive us. McKoy's technique includes the use of hand tools and power tools, as he says: 'I run the whole spectrum of hand tools, chisels, and power tools. There's nothing I won't use to remove wood. I'm not a classical sculptor.

Wood duck in a croker sack, 1993, basswood, tupelo and glass, 24in 610mm high

Nine quail, 1992, basswood, metal and glass, 48in 1220mm high

It's wood removal, but, it's an assembly process, too.' The birds eyes are constructed of glass.

Detail and design

'What catches people's eye is the detail,' says McKoy. He works life size to the larger dimensions of the species. 'Part of you wants to go close and look at it, to ponder and look at the detail, another part of you wants to back up and look at it as a whole piece. I want to inspire you and hope that you are drawn to it, another may want to back up and look at it for the design it presents. I hope to tug at you in two directions. Many people are convinced of one's mastery of a subject by the detail which is represented.'

McKoy works from sketches and models as well as the actual wildlife. Most of the large pieces take from ten to fourteen months: 'I work on one piece at a time on commission for individuals. They give me a space in which to work. The client may have seen some things I have done in the past. Some clients may like certain species. That's as far as it will go, I will take over from there.

> **'He advises artists to get to know their subject so they will not misrepresent it.'**

Someone may have a location on the coast and enjoy shorebirds, so it is no use producing or offering a design that has ducks in it. They give me a space and a vision of what they would like, but I take over the design and there is not much compromise on my part.'

Clients loan pieces for exhibits which may take place every ten years. The birds he carves are those he knows, including shorebirds, birds of prey and game birds. 'I feel uncomfortable reproducing things I'm not familiar with so I need to know the subject, I'm not going to compromise.' McKoy respects the wood: 'I am interested in wood and don't like to see it used improperly or cut unnecessarily. I think of stewardship when dealing with birds, wood or anything as a common thread through it all.' The sculptor's birds sing the praises of beauty and truth, eliciting a response in each of us. They are a rare expression of his gift.

Twenty-nine birds were recently represented, in his exhibition at the Brandywine River Museum, Chadds Ford, Pennsylvania. The works on display included single images of birds and large scale pieces of birds in flight. His works have been exhibited in museums, galleries and private collections in the USA. ■

CARVING A REALI...

DAVID TIPPEY

A SPECIALIST BIRD CARVER PROVIDES STEP-BY-STEP INSTRUCTIONS.

David Tippey took up woodworking and metalwork as a teenager, then later studied photography at Kitson College in Leeds.

He became the technical director of a Harrogate based electronics company but in 1984 changed career and moved to Kirkby Malham, in the Yorkshire Dales. A magazine article on American Decoys, prompted his first duck carvings in the American tradition.

In 1989 the opportunity arose to carve full time and, as his skills increased, his carvings moved away from the Decoy to subjects nearer home, and the creation of his own style.

He has two contrasting styles: highly detailed, textured realism, which he uses to capture mainly woodland and garden birds; and an elegant stylised form, drawing inspiration from the flowing shapes of wading birds and waterfowl. These stylised carvings provide a contrast to the meticulously worked carvings.

He also runs bird carving courses and is the organiser of the British Decoy & Wildfowl Carvers Association Northern Group.

The Subject

A delightful little bird to observe; perching on a branch, then swooping in a flash of black and white to catch the insects flying past. The choice of this bird as a subject was brought about by two factors: a pied flycatcher had nested behind my house last year, providing hours of enjoyment watching its aerobatics and also I was to attend 'Gwyl Adar 92', to be held at the RSPB Ynyshir Reserve near Machynlleth, where there would be about 100 pairs of nesting flycatchers to see.

The Working Drawing

When planning a carving, the first task is to collect together as much information as possible about the subject. I have several large ring files crammed with pictures of birds collected from magazines, postcards etc. These, along with the many bird books I have collected or borrow from libraries, provide the ideas for subjects and poses. My local museum also has a very good collection of cabinet skins and mounted birds, which are vital for getting accurate dimensional information.

Taxidermy mounts are not to be relied on for the overall shape of a subject but are used, in conjunction with photographs, to produce a basic working drawing for the bird, with as many measurements taken from the specimen as possible. The tip of the beak and the end of the tail are used as reference points for head and body measurements respectively. This practice would be frowned upon in the drawing office but birds are not 'precisely dimensioned components'. I keep a reference table of all the dimensions taken from the taxidermy mount, those which the taxidermist could not influence, to be referred to while carving. These dimensions have been included on the general drawings and can be used to produce an infinite variety of positions (see page 119).

The Model

The next step is to decide on the pose, in this case perched on a branch, looking for the next insect. Another possibility I considered was with an insect or caterpillar in its beak, but time did not allow.

If a natural branch is to be used then this must be found before you go any further. I collect interesting branches and pieces of driftwood constantly, usually picking them up when walking the dog. The piece of branch chosen for this carving was cleaned with hot soapy water and a stiff scrubbing brush and then bleached with a proprietary two part wood bleach. This gives a stark white branch which can be toned down when the piece is painted.

The reference photographs now come into use. If you can sketch well, you can play about with different angles and poses of bird and branch.

Not being able to draw well, but having rather better modelling abilities, I choose to make a full size model, which enables me to view the subject from all angles and make adjustments. A model is still worth making even if you can draw, because it can be viewed from all angles, is easily altered and becomes your reference for carving.

I use plasticine for the body and head of the model, mounted on a square ended dowel. The beak is carved from dowel, the eyes are glass on wire and thin card is used to form wings and tail. The card parts are cut out to the working drawing previously made, and several holes are punched through the card to allow the modelling clay to key on the surface. You cannot put fine details onto the model; it is used only to get the overall shape and surface form. I use well polished stainless steel wax modelling tools,[1] constantly wiping them clean on a cloth to prevent the clay sticking. It is easy to turn the head or tail or raise a wing to alter the overall composition. I refer to the branch while creating the model, as it is part of the final composition, and try to get as much animation as possible into the stance of the bird.

The dimensions of the finished model are checked for accuracy against the measurements on the drawing, paying particular attention to the head, eye and beak dimensions. A well-shaped head, in a lively attitude will give life to the carving and take attention away from minor imperfections in the body or feather carving.

The model is now ready to make the patterns from and then to be used as a full three-dimensional reference when carving.

The Pattern

The model is put belly down on a piece of thick card, and supported so that the tail and the plane, through the widest parts of the carving, lie horizontal. A small set square is then moved up to the model until it just touches and a pencil mark is tranferred to the card at the heel of the square. This is repeated all around the model until enough points have been transferred. An alternative homemade device for drawing the patterns is shown in the

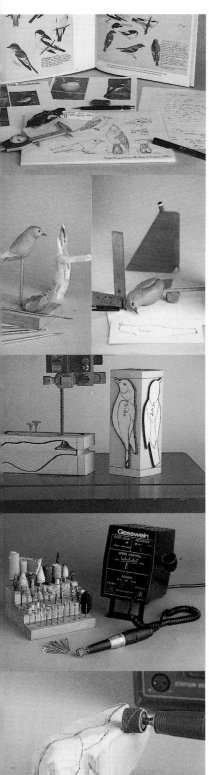

1. The information collected to produce the working drawing

2. The plasticene model, with the prepared branch

3. Making the card pattern. Note the alternative device for transferring the model's shape to the card

4. Marking out and bandsawing the side view on the re-assembled block

5. The high-speed grinder and tools used to carve the flycatcher. The tool blocks contain HS steel and carbide cutters, ruby and diamond abrasive burrs and small grindstones

6. Roughing out the blank with a small sanding drum

7. Rounding up the blank to define the overall shape

illustrations. The line joining all these points is then drawn and the top view pattern cut out. The model is now set up on its side in the same manner, and a pattern formed for the side elevation. I allow extra material around head and bill areas, and extra thickness on the tail when cutting the pattern out.

Tools

Realistic bird carving uses one or two tools not usually owned by wood carvers. On a small carving like this, I will carry out almost all the work with a small high-speed electric grinder rather like a dentist's drill. I use an American Gesswein grinder,[2] which will run at speeds up to 55,000 rpm in either direction, so that you do not have to work against the grain. It has a convenient quick change collet system to allow the tools to be changed in seconds. I use it with a large variety of $\frac{1}{8}$″ and $\frac{3}{32}$″ shank cutting burrs and grinding points, to shape and texture the carving. On larger carvings, I use a heavier more powerful Pfingst flexible shaft carving machine[2][3] which will take large $\frac{1}{4}$″ shank burrs and cutters. Drawknives, spokeshaves and gouges are also used for shaping large carvings prior to detailing and texturing.

Use of power carving techniques allows the carving to be performed without too much regard for the effects of grain in the blank; and enables soft feathers to be created which would be impossible to do with edge tools. Other power carving tools are also suitable. On a small project like this, reasonable detailing and texturing could be achieved with a high speed, modeller's mini-drill. The other essential tool needed is a pyrograph, not the crude soldering iron type but one with scalpel like handpieces with a variable heat control.[2]

Timber

Three timbers are available in the United Kingdom, which are suitable for the feather carving

techniques used to produce realistic bird carvings: lime, jelutong and basswood.[2][3]

The characteristics looked for are relative ease of carving, lack of knots and a homogenous texture (pronounced hard and soft annual growth rings texture and burn unevenly). Jelutong produces very fine dust when worked, which some people find is an irritant: it also contains latex canals which have to be avoided when cutting out the blank.

Lime and basswood are similar types of timber, both work very well with edge tools but can tend to fuzz up when worked with grinding cutters. Basswood and lime are much tougher than jelutong in thin sections. The choice is yours, all three are used successfully by many bird carvers, I usually use lime or basswood for small carvings and have decided to use basswood for the flycatcher.

The Blank

The top view pattern is drawn centrally on a square section block, the end points of the pattern are then transferred round the block using a try square. The side view is now drawn on the block, aligned to the squared pencil lines, the extra $\frac{1}{16}$″ or so added around the head when making the pattern, is necessary because after bandsawing it is a rather odd shape and needs trimming to regain the correct head shape. It is easy to remove too much timber at this stage. The timber block needs to be big enough, I try to leave a $\frac{1}{4}$″ to $\frac{3}{8}$″ between the pattern and the edge of the block.

The side view is now carefully bandsawed, keeping the off cuts. When the side view has been completely cut, re-assemble the whole block using pins, tape or hot melt glue and then carefully cut out the top view. The result will be an odd, but vaguely bird shaped piece of wood. The head in particular will be badly mis-shapen if it has been turned by

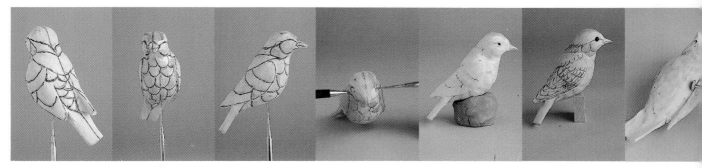

more than a few degrees to the side.

Carving

The blank now needs to be roughed to shape, firstly pencil in the three centre lines of the head, body and tail. This is made easier by the use of a flexible plastic ruler or any piece of celluloid or similar material with a straight edge. If the centre lines are removed at any stage of carving replace them; they are a valuable aid to maintaining the correct shape.

I now mark out the areas of the blank that need removing; constant reference to the clay model helps with this. The head area in particular needs very careful marking out, as it is very easy to end up with too little wood by the time you have corrected the head shape.

I start by removing the waste around the wings and tail with a small sanding drum. Remove the wood in square steps at this stage, and don't start to round up yet. The small block on the head which will later become the beak, is defined. I then start by looking at the tip of the beak, square to the front and along the centre-line of the head. You can see that the top of the head is higher on the side that is turned into the body. I remove only the high spot that can be seen, then tilt the beak downwards slightly and sight along the centreline again, and repeat. This process is continued until I have reshaped all the top of the head.

Now viewing the head from the top, using the drawings and model, I transfer the shape of the head to the block; this will determine the waste areas in the neck region. I can now finish roughing out the head area, leaving a blank which now resembles a squared up version

of the clay model. The shape is then rounded up using a flame-shaped carbide cutter, referring constantly to the model as work progresses.

Feather groups are marked out on the wing and body, the wing groups are defined by referring to the working drawing, the body groups are slightly more arbitrary and blend with the body shape and the flow of the feathers.

These feather groups, or slight bumps as they will become when carved, break the surface of the carving into a more interesting form, so that when the feathers are carved the effect will be soft and slightly puffed up.

The feather groups are outlined with a ¼" diameter, round cutter and then blended into the surrounding area. The overall shape can now be seen, so before any detailing work is done on the body, the head is carved.

All the work up to this point could be whittled with a knife and small gouge, but from this point on in the work a rotary tool is really needed.

The beak was carved first, roughed out a little over size, from the small block left on the head when shaping up initially. I used a ¼" cylindrical diamond cutter for this, carefully checking the measurements as I carved.

The eye position was then drawn in on one side of the head and the position then transferred to the other side. This is done by sighting. I put the point of an awl to the first eye position and present the point of a pencil to the

other side. The pencil is aligned with the awl looking from the front of the head, and a horizontal line drawn. The pencil point is then aligned from the top of the head and a second vertical line drawn to give the eye centre position.

The eye centres are checked for visual alignment and then holes are drilled (⅛" diameter) from each side. They should meet in the middle; the drill bit or a nail can be put through the two holes to check they are horizontal and at right angles to the centre line of the head.

The eye channel, check and ear coverts are now marked out and the eye channel is carved. The eye to eye distance is made just

slightly more than shown on the drawing to allow for sanding and texturing. The eye hole is enlarged to take a 4mm diameter eye, then the check and ear covert groups are formed. These areas are then blended together to give the final head shape. The whole bird is now sanded to blend all the feather groups and give a smooth surface to mark the feathers on.

Feather Carving and Burning

The feathers are now pencilled in on both wings, using the drawing as reference. They are relieved with a cylindrical stone or diamond burr, then sanded (emery board nail files are good for this).

The wings are parted from the body slightly using a diamond

8/10. The main feather groups marked out and carved

11. Marking out the eye centres

12. Feather groups carved and sanded, ready for marking out individual feathers

13. Individual feathers pencilled in

14. Separating wing from body

18. Pyrograph, with the handpieces used in the carving

19. Burning the feather barbs, note the angle of the burning pen

20. Feather flow guidelines pencilled in

21. Head textured with conical stone

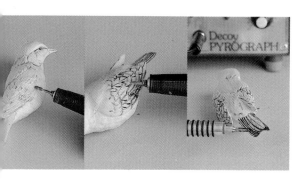

15. Carving wing feathers with abrasive stone

16. Grinding in ripples and large feather splits

17. Defining the edge of the tail feathers with the pyrograph

22. Legs temporarily fitted and tried on branch

rotor saw, and the excess material removed from under the wings. The upper rump and the areas under the wings where they join the body are brought to shape using a pointed diamond burr.

The tail feathers are now drawn in and relieved in the same way as the wing feathers.

The edges of the tail feathers and the primaries can be defined more clearly by burning the edge of the feathers with a pyrograph, the handpiece held almost flat on the surface of the feathers. This process can also be used to relieve feathers too close for grinding satisfactorily.

The pyrograph[2] is a form of heated scalpel, the temperature is variable and many different handpieces are available. The handpiece is kept clean and sharp by stropping on a piece of leather dressed with Autosol chrome cleaner, in the same way as a knife.

Breaks in the feathers are the next to be pencilled in and then ground into the feather using a small pointed stone. The same stone can be used to put small ripples on the surface of each feather, running in the direction of the feather barbs.

The feather shafts are marked out then burned with the pyrograph on a low heat setting. They are burned from both sides, the pyrograph point inclined at about 45 degrees to the feather surface. Feather shafts should not be too heavy, it is better to err on the thin side and a single line may be sufficient on a small feather.

Feather barbs are burned next, at a slightly higher setting. The burning tool needs to be sharp and held perpendicular to the surface of the feather. The lines are not straight but curved slightly towards the tip of the feather. This is achieved by twisting the handpiece slightly between the fingers while burning

the lines. More fine feather splits can be added with the burning tool. Some feathers can be separated and given a slightly lifted appearance by burning at an angle underneath the edge of the feather.

Texturing

The feathers that have been carved, burned and textured so far are the ones which are individually discernible on the bird, they can be considered to be 'hard edged'. On the rest of the bird the feathers are soft and flow together, individual feathers can not be picked out. These areas are textured on this carving.

The flow of the feathers over the head and body is drawn as a series of lines on the carving. It is especially important to get the directions correct, as these pencilled lines are then used as a guide for the texturing.

The texturing is done using small abrasive stones. Short wavy lines are ground into the surface following the flow lines laid down in pencil. On smooth feather areas like the head, all the stoning is done with a small inverted cone point; where a coarser texture is required, on the breast for example, a base texture is ground in first using a larger cylindrical stone.

The base texture can take the form of feather shapes which, when textured over, will give the impression of individual feathers. The texturing needs to be done thoroughly, going over areas several times, one feather group at a time. Nothing looks worse than just an odd few lines barely covering the surface of the carving.

The effect of the texturing is now made even softer by going over the textured areas with the pyrograph pen on a fairly low setting. Occasionally one or two lines are burned deeper, using a higher setting, and the edge of one or two feathers is defined by burning.

Legs and Eyes

The legs are then fitted. Cast pewter legs imported from America were used,[2][3] so a suitably-sized pair had to be selected. If suitable ones are unavailable, legs and feet can be made of brass wire, soldered

together and then ground to shape; or a suitable cast foot can be cut off and used with a brass wire leg.

The holes are marked out on the carving and then drilled, checking with the drawing to make sure that the mechanics of the leg would physically allow the leg to get to the position marked. The corresponding holes on the branch are marked out and drilled and the carving tried in place. If the hole in the carving is enlarged within the body, using a small ball shaped cutter, then some adjustment, is possible. If all is satisfactory then the leg holes in the body cavity are packed with stick epoxy putty,[2][3] the legs inserted and aligned and the carving set aside overnight to set.

The eyes are fitted at the same time; the eye holes had previously been carved so that a 4mm black glass ball eye[2] would fit. Epoxy putty is packed into the eye socket and the eye inserted wire first. The eye is then pushed back using a piece of dowel or the eraser end of a pencil. (The eye must be seated deep enough or else the bird will look 'pop-eyed'.) The excess putty squeezed out in the process is removed.

When the epoxy putty has set, eyelids are formed using plastic wood. A small fillet of plastic wood is put around the eye, only a little is needed. It is thoroughly wetted with Acetone and the fillet evened up using a brush.

The eye opening is shaped using a small pointed sable brush. This process is then repeated on the other eye; the eyelid remains workable as long as the plastic wood is well wetted with solvent. When the surface of the plastic wood has formed a skin, I use a small dental tool to gently press around the eye to form the eye ring. Eyelids can also be formed from thin rolls of epoxy putty but it is more difficult to get two the same.

Plastic wood is also used to form a small tuft of feathers around the leg, where it leaves the body, again it is worked to shape with a brush and solvent. Plastic wood can be textured when dry, or burned with a pyrograph on low heat.

The beak is carved to final size and shape, using a small bullet shaped grinding stone and the

23. Completed carving and base ready for painting

24. Carving attached to a stick for painting, the breast is painted and the 'black' areas sketched in

25. The finished piece

separation between the upper and lower mandibles and the nostril holes formed with the pyrograph. The texturing around the beak is completed, then the beak and the tips of the tail and wing feathers are soaked in thin superglue to toughen them.

The carving is brushed with a soft toothbrush, to remove the dust and carbon from the texturing, before sealing with several coats of well-thinned cellulose sanding sealer. When the sealer is fully dry, I brush the carving, following the texturing, with a stiff rotary bristle brush run slowly. This removes any fuzziness caused by wood fibres left attached to the carving.

The Base

A base was turned from a piece of burr elm, leaving a natural edge at one point. It was turned down until the natural area matched the width of the branch base. The base was then polished and the branch attached using epoxy adhesive. The joint was reinforced by a woodscrew driven into the base of the branch, the head cut off leaving about 1" stuck out, and glued into a pre-drilled hole.

The area where the branch and natural edge of the base met was then tidied up with some carving and a little plastic wood and the branch sealed with thinned cellulose sanding sealer. The

natural area on the base ties it into the composition, the base and branch 'growing' together. The depression in the top of the base was then covered in catalysed woodfiller which was textured by stippling with a brush just before it set.

Painting

The carving is temporarily attached to a drilled wooden stick, using superglue. This enables it to be held while painting. It is first given a couple of coats of thinned acrylic gesso, applied with a stiff hogs hair brush following the direction of the feather barbs and texturing. Care must be taken not to use too much paint or it will fill up the texturing and burning lines. Heat cannot be used to speed up the drying of the gesso.

The carving is painted with artists' acrylic paints. Any make can be used but the paint should only be applied in very thin washes so that the texturing does not fill up with pigment. A hair drier can be used to speed up drying of the colour washes. I mainly use an acrylic gouache by Jo Sonja,[2][3] which gives a nice even matt finish.

The breast is painted first with washes of titanium white. The shaded area under the feather groups is created by blending in thin washes of nimbus grey; the centres of the feather groups have warm white blended into them. The blending is done by dampening the area to be worked with clean water, then adding the new colour with an almost dry brush. Feather edge highlights are added with titanium white using a sable brush with the hair trained into a flat fan. The whole breast area is then given a very thin wash of nimbus grey. This process leaves the breast area with several different values of white. The shading under the feather groups adds to the puffed up appearance of the feathers.

The 'black' areas of the head, back, wings, tail and upper rump are then sketched in using a very thin wash of Rowney ultramarine blue. The bird is first dampened with clean water. Corrections can then be made to the edge of the black area by using a clean damp brush. These 'black' areas are

then painted with thin washes of Rowney ultramarine blue and burnt sienna; starting with a 50:50 mix, the colour can be varied easily. More sienna gives a warmer brown black, more ultramarine a colder blue black. These two colours are used to provide an infinite variety of brown and black values in bird painting.

The head, cape and upper tail are painted a blue black colour, the primaries are more brownish in hue, several values of each colour are used. The subtle variations of hue within a colour add to the softness and realism. To get the final depth of colour required, ten or more washes may be needed.

The quills of the white wing feathers are painted warm white with a liner brush, and the black quills carbon black. Under the wing and tail feathers are given a couple of washes of the black mix with burnt umber added, this leaves them a whitish brown. The quills on these feathers are painted with this mix with white added. Feet are washed burnt umber then a final wash with the blue black mix. The claws and the eye ring are straight black, and the beak is the blue black mix. Finally the quills, beak and feet are given several coats of thinned matt medium which, despite its name, gives them a gloss finish.

The branch is blended into the natural area of the base using burnt umber, then several washes of pale grey are used to give a more weathered appearance. The brown catalysed filler was given several different washes of green and brown earth colours, and then the bird was finally glued in position. ∎

Suppliers for special items mentioned in the text:
[1] Proops Bros, 21 Mason Avenue, Wealdstone, Harrow, Middlesex.
[2] Pintail Carving, 20 Sheppenhall Grove, Aston, Nantwich, Cheshire.
[3] Old Hall Decoys, Old Hall Farm, Scole, Diss, Norfolk.

A kit containing a selected bandsawn lime or basswood blank cut to the pattern in this article, complete with suitable legs and eyes, is available from the author:
[4] David Tippey, Victoria Lodge, Kirkby Malham, Nr Skipton, N. Yorks BD23 4BS. Tel. 0729 830547.

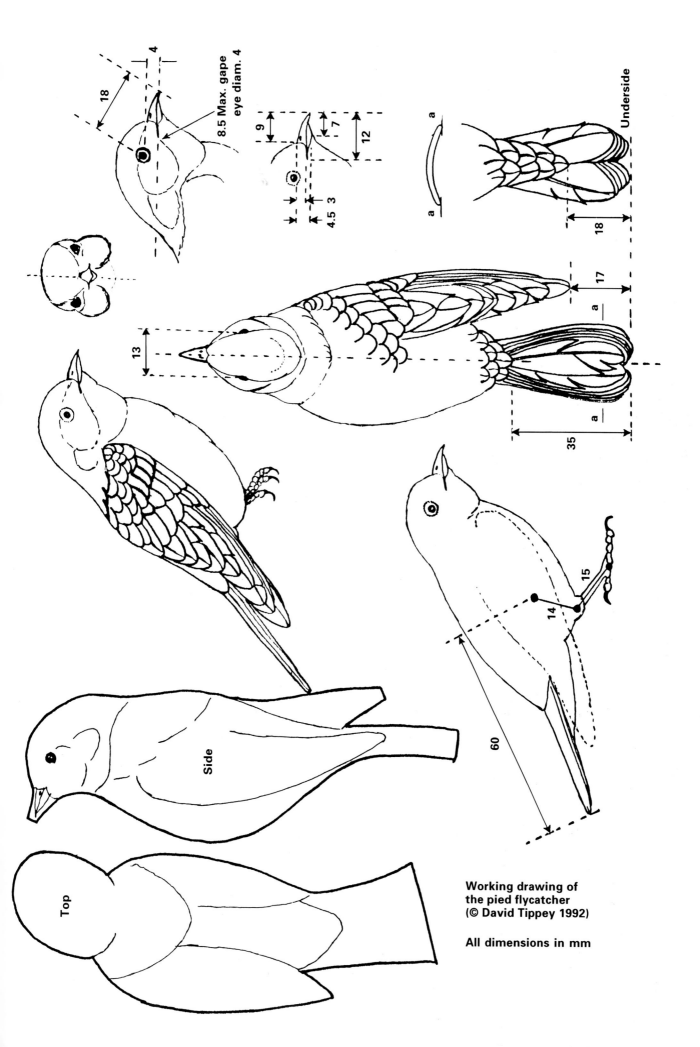

8.5 Max. gape
eye diam. 4

Underside

Side

Top

Working drawing of
the pied flycatcher
(© David Tippey 1992)

All dimensions in mm

INDEX